All about us, in earth and air,
wherever the eye or ear can reach,
there is a power ever breathing itself forth in signs,
now in daisy, now in a wind-waft, a cloud, a sunset;
a power that holds constant and sweetest relation
with the dark and silent world within us.
The same God who is in us,
and upon whose tree we are the buds,
if not yet the flowers,
also is all about us —
inside, the Spirit;
outside, the Word.
And the two are ever trying to meet in us;
and when they meet, then the sign without,
and the longing within, become one in light,
and the man no more walketh in darkness,
but knoweth whither he goeth.

George MacDonald,
Thomas Wingfold

Recently discovered photograph of MacDonald, circa 1870.

THE HARMONY WITHIN

The Spiritual Vision of
George MacDonald

BY ROLLAND HEIN

CHRISTIAN
UNIVERSITY
PRESS

A SUBSIDIARY OF CHRISTIAN COLLEGE CONSORTIUM
AND WM. B. EERDMANS PUBLISHING COMPANY,
GRAND RAPIDS, MICHIGAN

Available from Wm. B. Eerdmans Publishing Co.
255 Jefferson Ave., S.E., Grand Rapids, Mich. 49503

Library of Congress Cataloging in Publication Data

Hein, Rolland.
  The harmony within.

  Bibliography: p. 156
    1. MacDonald, George, 1824-1905 —Religion and ethics.
2. Christianity in literature. 3. Myth in literature.
4. Fantastic fiction, English —History and criticism.
5. Children's stories, English —History and criticism.
I. Title.
PR4969.H44 1982   823'.8   82-1488
ISBN 0-8028-1912-5 (Eerdmans)   AACR2

To Mother and Dad

*From whom I first learned to
love the good and the true*

ACKNOWLEDGMENTS

I would like to express appreciation to Harold H. Watts, Professor Emeritus of Purdue University, for wisely and patiently helping to shape my early responses to MacDonald's art; to the Alumni Association of Wheaton College for a grant to enable me to work on this project; to Jack Clark, Associate Professor of Spanish at Wheaton College, for reading the manuscript and offering advice; and to Mrs. Betty Boardman for graciously typing the manuscript. Portions of this book have appeared in somewhat altered form in *Faith and Fiction: A Study of the Effects of Religious Convictions in the Adult Fantasies and Novels of George MacDonald*, Diss. Purdue University 1971; "Lilith: Theology through Mythopoeia," *Christian Scholar's Review*, 3 (1974), 215-231; and "If You Would But Write Novels, Mr. MacDonald," *Seven*, 1 (1980), 11-27. Reprinted by permission.

The author and publisher also wish to thank Johnson Reprints (a division of Harcourt Brace Jovanovich) for permission to reprint excerpts from Greville MacDonald's *George MacDonald & His Wife* (1971). Four of the photographs used are also taken from this biography: cover picture (also used on p. v); top right photograph, p. vi; bottom photograph, p. vi; photograph, p. viii. Another four of the photographs used are from the archives of the Marion E. Wade Collection, Wheaton College, Wheaton, Illinois: frontispiece; bottom photograph, p. i; top left photograph, p. vi; top photograph, p. vii. The remainder of the pictures were taken by the author on his trip overseas in the summer of 1979.

TABLE OF CONTENTS

vii

INTRODUCTION

"Where are ye going?" a voice with a strong Scotch accent inquires of the narrator in C. S. Lewis's *The Great Divorce*, a fantasy of heaven and hell. The narrator, wandering through the nether world, tells how he turned to see an "enthroned and shining god, whose ageless spirit weighed upon mine like a burden of solid gold: and yet, at the very same moment, here was an old weather-beaten man, one who might have been a shepherd." When the inquirer identifies himself as George MacDonald, the narrator is beside himself with joy. He cries, " 'Then you can tell me! You at least will not deceive me.' " He then explains his confidence:

> . . . I tried, trembling, to tell this man all that his writings had done for me. I tried to tell how a certain frosty afternoon at Leatherhead Station when I first bought a copy of Phantastes (being then about sixteen years old) had been to me what the first sight of Beatrice had been to Dante: Here begins the New Life. I started to confess how long that Life had delayed in the region of imagination merely: how slowly and reluctantly I had come to admit that his Christendom had more than an accidental connexion with it, how hard I had tried not to see that the true name of the quality which first met me in his books is Holiness. [1]

After humbly receiving this homage, MacDonald becomes the narrator's teacher, explaining to him many difficult truths about heaven and hell.

Lewis chose his guide well. He owed George MacDonald a large spiritual debt, and, in his many writings, often acknowledged MacDonald as his master. C. S. Lewis is, of course, one of the leading Christian apologists of our century, but many of

---

[1] *The Great Divorce* (New York: Macmillan, 1946), pp. 60-61. Italics his. For Lewis's more complete explanation of his debt to MacDonald, see *Surprised by Joy* (New York: Harcourt, 1955), and the Preface to *George MacDonald: An Anthology* (New York: Macmillan, 1948), pp. 10-22, hereafter cited as *Anthology*. The latter is an excellent summary of MacDonald's life and achievement.

his ideas are to be found first in MacDonald's writings. These two men never met, Lewis's life spanning the first half of the twentieth century and MacDonald's the latter three-fourths of the nineteenth, but MacDonald wrote prolifically, and Lewis became quite familiar with his work. This familiarity also taught Lewis many valuable lessons in the art of writing fantasy, for MacDonald was a master of this literary type.[2] He wrote fantasies not merely for entertainment — and not for direct instruction, either. Rather, MacDonald's intention was by symbolic suggestion to penetrate eternal reality. Many readers seem to feel he has succeeded, at least to the extent of arousing within them longings after truth and goodness.

As Lewis's narrator has said, his first encounter with the reality that MacDonald defines began in the realm of the imagination, and from there permeated his life. MacDonald firmly believed that it is through the imagination that man may reach farthest toward truth. Certainly his many prose fantasies, children's fairy tales, and some two dozen long Victorian novels attest to the strength of his conviction that literary art can be spiritually valuable to man. He writes in his novel, *Paul Faber, Surgeon*: "It is God who gives thee thy mirror of imagination and if thou keep it clean, it will give thee back no shadow but the truth."

MacDonald's mirror was clean. Few people in the history of man have had a larger vision of the beauty of holiness and goodness than he, and few have succeeded as he did in communicating the attraction to goodness that good men feel. He is a moralist, certainly, and of the sternest order, but to classify him as such is to put him in the company of many vastly unlike himself. The stilted, negative preachiness that identifies the type

[2]I am using the term *fantasy* in the sense defined by Colin Nicholas Manlove in *Modern Fantasy: Five Studies* (Cambridge: Cambridge University Press, 1975), p. 1: "A fiction evoking wonder and containing a substantial and irreducible element of the supernatural with which the mortal characters in the story or the readers become on at least partly familiar terms." He elaborates upon the characteristics of this genre in his Introduction.

in our minds, the long-faced Puritan's suspicion of all that is enjoyable or beautiful — these are completely foreign to him. To MacDonald, goodness alone is joyous; God's will alone is our best good. Writing a birthday greeting to his physician son, Greville, in 1887, he counsels: "To be one with him [God] seems the only common sense, as well as the only peace. Let him do with you, my beloved son, as he wills. Be hearty with his will. Submission is not the right feeling when we say 'Thy will be done.' His will is the only good. . . ."[3] To one with this attitude, life is an adventure toward fullness of being, and hence of joy. But self-abnegation, together with purity of heart and a child-like spirit of confidence and wonder in the presence of the universal mystery of things, is necessary to achieve the desired oneness with God. All MacDonald's writings convey these convictions.

This is not to say that MacDonald overlooked evil in the world or within man, or that he did not advocate social reform. Through MacDonald's long life he knew firsthand the hardships and embarrassments of poverty, the pain and depression of disease, and the heartache caused by the deaths of loved ones. He saw the amassing of money by the few as having most dire consequences, both on individuals and on society. But he celebrates in his writings the capacity of the individual human spirit, allied with the Spirit of God and drawing upon eternal resources, to triumph over all. He does not minimize present distress, but he does point beyond to the good that may certainly develop.

Just as he takes no simple view of the nature of evil, neither

[3]Greville MacDonald, *George MacDonald and His Wife* (New York: Dial, 1924), p. 535. This biography is the chief source of material on MacDonald's life. It is a competently, but somewhat heavily, written family history, compiled of letters written by and to George MacDonald, reminiscences of friends and admirers, and personal recollections of the author. As one might expect, the book praises its subjects highly, and might be called biased — but its contains a wealth of information. Hereafter, references to it in the text will be cited as *GMDW*. Greville also makes some scattered references to his father in his autobiography *Reminiscences of a Specialist* (London: George Allen & Unwin, 1932), hereafter cited as *ROS*.

does he take a simple view of the nature of spiritual experience. In a day when so much Christian thought seems shallow and inadequate, bent as it is on reducing Christian prescriptions for human experience into simple formulas and four-step patterns, MacDonald reminds us how complex are our spiritual plights and how many-faceted is the truth. He does not involve us in classifying our experiences or in stifling them; he teaches us, rather, to honor our individuality and uniqueness before God. He sees a glory and a cause for wonder in all the simple, unsought feelings of man, and he is earnestly concerned that they all be related to goodness.

The concern that his imaginative writings reveal is, of course, often clothed in imagery drawn from the Victorian world and Victorian literary conventions. He is a captive of his times, as we all are of our own. Unfortunately, it is the children's stories and fairy tales that are most affected by the social organization and manners of the times, so that the average child of today may hardly understand them, having little in his own experience that is comparable. But the value of this children's literature is by no means lost upon the adult reader who, fascinated by the adult fantasies of *Phantastes* and *Lilith*, turns to them for additional imaginative depictions of MacDonald's provocative spiritual insights. Such readers find some of his memorable scenes in these tales, particularly in those that are book-length: *At the Back of the North Wind*, *The Princess and Curdie*, and *The Princess and the Goblin*. No less a man than G. K. Chesterton said of the latter that it changed his "whole existence," helping him "to see things in a certain way from the start" (*GMDW*, p. 9).[4]

Chesterton's strong praise is typical of MacDonald's devotees, an appreciable group in his own time and one that, judging from the contemporary emergence of reprints and editions of his

[4]For MacDonald's influence upon Chesterton, see Leo A. Hetzler, "George MacDonald and G. K. Chesterton," *Durham University Journal*, 37 (1976), 176-182.

Introduction

works, is a growing coterie today. In his own day, MacDonald was an esteemed acquaintance of several noted writers: Tennyson, Arnold, and Ruskin, to name but three.[5] He also developed a wide following among the more pietistic Christian laity in England and America, his works having a wide market and being avidly read. Yet, with the exception of a series of printed adulations at the time of his death and later at the celebration of his centenary — which was led by his devoted son Greville in 1924 — only desultory attention was accorded him until relatively recent times. Sharing C. S. Lewis's deep admiration of his work was W. H. Auden, who held MacDonald in high esteem. He described him as "preeminently a mythopoeic writer" of "very considerable literary gifts" who, "in his power to project his inner life into images, events, beings, landscapes which are valid for all . . . is one of the most remarkable writers of the nineteenth century."[6] This power is what helps to give his work a spiritual consistency, a "harmony within."

Both Auden and Lewis, however, are careful to qualify their praise by pointing out the painfully obvious fault of prolix and facile sermonizing which burdens so much of MacDonald's fiction. This is not to say that his interspersed sermonic passages are not fine as sermons, capable of large appeal to those who appreciate this species of writing. But they simply act as a weight upon much of his fiction, even to the extent of obscuring the moral insights that would otherwise be manifest to a larger group of readers today. The *Athenaeum*, in an appreciative obituary,

[5]An often-reprinted plate of an assemblage of eight Victorians shows MacDonald in company with Thackery, Macaulay, Bulwer-Lytton, Carlyle, Dickens, Froude, Collins, and Trollope. Richard H. Reis, *George MacDonald* (New York: Twayne, 1972), p. 17, sees this as a "composite photograph" with "an apparently sketched-in background." Nevertheless, many of MacDonald's contemporaries considered him a part of the company of such literati.

[6]Introduction, *The Visionary Novels of George MacDonald*, Anne Fremantle, ed. (New York: Noonday, 1954), pp. v-vi.

noted with characteristic British retraint that his novels are "too consciously didactic to attain great success perhaps."[7]

Critical attention to MacDonald has increased of late. In addition to various dissertations, two book-length studies have appeared. One is entitled *The Golden Key*, written by Robert Lee Wolff. His work is provocative, and the scholarship astute, particularly his tracing of sources and his delineation of certain influences upon MacDonald's thought and production. Mr. Wolff, however, uses a Freudian approach to the fantasies and novels, and the result, however clever in its own way, does little to illuminate the literary merit of the works themselves. For example, with characteristic Freudian relentlessness, he found a letter written by MacDonald's mother at the time of his weaning which attests to her grief at his crying, and which the adult MacDonald kept among other precious family trifles in his desk. This letter, Wolff asserts, offers "a clue to George MacDonald's character and writing that we shall find invaluable at almost every turn."[8] The mother's firmness dealt her child a "wound that never healed," a claim Wolff uses throughout his book to account for many of MacDonald's attitudes. This kind of thinking also produces his curious interpretation of MacDonald's charming fairy tale "The Golden Key," in which the child Mossy finds a golden key at the foot of the rainbow and goes in search of the one keyhole he is told it will unlock. When in the end Mossy finds the keyhole and with his companion Tangle opens the door with the key, the two joyfully climb a stair leading from earth

[7]Obituary of Sept. 23, 1905, p. 400, as quoted by John Malcolm Bulloch in "A Bibliography of George MacDonald," *Aberdeen University Library Bulletin*, 5, No. 30 (February 1925), 734. This annotated bibliography, contained in pp. 679-747, is particularly valuable to the student of MacDonald, providing information that is otherwise very difficult to obtain. It lists all editions of primary material published in England and some in America, together with a list of various "Appreciations" that appeared up until the centenary. Muriel Hutton offers some corrections of Bulloch's work in "Sour Grapeshot: Fault-finding in *A Centennial Bibliography of George MacDonald*," *Aberdeen University Review*, 41, No. 134 (Autumn 1965), 85-88.

[8]*The Golden Key: A Study of the Fiction of George MacDonald* (New Haven: Yale University Press, 1961), pp. 12-13; hereafter cited as *GK*.

Introduction

to a beautiful country above. To Wolff, the most satisfying interpretation is that Mossy's key is his phallus; he reads the adventures of the quest primarily in sexual terms. Thus a story of
charm and beauty quickly is made to seem coarse and ludicrous.
The shortcomings of Wolff's approach are those of Freudian
literary criticism in general: not only is the focus of attention
diverted from the literary work to the psychological disposition
of the author, presenting him in a highly speculative light, but
also little help is given to the student who wants to measure
literary achievement.

Mr. Wolff's interpretation is well answered in the work of
Richard H. Reis,[9] who has written a helpful general introduction
to MacDonald's imaginative prose. He measures MacDonald's
literary achievement from a more traditional point of view. In
addition, two critics have devoted some attention to MacDonald's
work in their treatment of subjects to which MacDonald's
achievement is *apropos*. In his *Modern Fantasy*, Colin Nicholas
Manlove considers some aspects of MacDonald's thought and
certain of his fantasies, and is generally unimpressed.[10] More
appreciative treatments appear in Stephen Prickett's *Romanticism
and Religion: The Tradition of Coleridge and Wordsworth in the Victorian
Church*, and his *Victorian Fantasy*.[11] Professor Prickett shows how
closely MacDonald adheres, in his creation of fantasy worlds, to
Coleridge's theory of the nature and function of symbols, and
how MacDonald's mysticism makes him distinctive.

[9]*George MacDonald* (New York: Twayne, 1972).

[10]*Modern Fantasy: Five Studies* (Cambridge: Cambridge University Press,
1975). Manlove's chapter on MacDonald is an expansion of his article
"George MacDonald's Fairy Tales: Their Roots in MacDonald's Thought"
in *Studies in Scottish Literature*, 8 (1970), 97-108. Manlove alleges various
contradictions in MacDonald's thought and tends to dismiss the resolutions
MacDonald attempts. Cf. Reis: "Although MacDonald himself never really
put forward his ideas as a coherent system, a close examination of his
scattered philosophical remarks has convinced me that they all arise from
a systematic, consistent set of beliefs" (p. 31). MacDonald's thought certainly may be faulted, but not, I think, for inconsistency.

[11]*Romanticism and Religion* (Cambridge: Cambridge University Press,
1976); *Victorian Fantasy* (Bloomington: Indiana University Press, 1979).

What is presently needed in MacDonald studies is a demonstration of how his beliefs create a "harmony within" — how thoroughly the symbolic terrain of his imaginative prose is shaped by his theological convictions, and hence by his understanding of the Bible. This is what I am undertaking. MacDonald was a devout and careful student of the Christian Scriptures, and his imagination, consciously and unconsciously, was shaped by them. With this truth as a guide I hope to illuminate much (not all) of the obscurity of the fantasies. I am not directly concerned with measuring literary quality as such, although I will offer various judgments along the way. Others — notably Lewis and Reis — have evaluated MacDonald's literary qualities, and there is little point in my repeating their opinions.

Many readers of MacDonald's fantasies are profoundly affected by them, and they are curious about the source and nature of this influence. What affects them is the insight into what are felt to be the ultimate truths about existence, conceived from a Christian point of view. MacDonald achieves this mythic impact with symbolism. His art is seldom allegorical, infrequently presenting the rather rigid and mechanical relation between select images and their abstract significances that one finds, say, in *Pilgrim's Progress*.[12] Rather, his work is symbolical, in the sense that an image or scene only suggests a theme or idea: some truth about life and experience informs the imagery, giving it shape. Because the particular truth being handled is elusive and obscure by its very nature, the symbolic image adumbrates it, as a metaphor would not. The symbol does not — it cannot — capture or

[12]In his essay "The Fantastic Imagination," MacDonald writes: "A fairytale is not an allegory. There may be an allegory in it, but it is not an allegory. He must be an artist indeed who can, in any mode, produce a strict allegory that is not a weariness to the spirit." This essay first appeared as the Preface to the 1893 American edition of *The Light Princess and Other Fairy Tales*, and was also included in *A Dish of Orts: Chiefly Papers on the Imagination, and on Shakespeare*, enl. ed. (London, 1893), pp. 313-22; hereafter cited as *ADO*. It is also reprinted in Glen Edward Sadler, ed., *The Gifts of the Child Christ: Fairy Tales and Stories for the Childlike* (Grand Rapids, Mich.: Wm. B. Eerdmans, 1973).

Introduction

imprison the insight so as to define it precisely and hence to exhaust its meaning. For instance, the image of a fire burning in the shape of beautiful roses, as does the great-great-grand-mother's fire in *The Princess and the Goblin*, tells us something otherwise unstateable about the nature of the holiness of God that loves unto purity. Art may function in this way, helping us glimpse what the mind has not otherwise discerned, and, when the glimpse is momentarily in focus, arousing a profound intuitive response deep within us.

This type of literary art is generally termed mythic today. Myth is possibly the oldest of literary genres, reaching as it does back into primordial time, having sprung from the collective unconscious of earliest man. The ancient mythologies were imaginative attempts to account for the inscrutable nature of the universe, myths sustained by man's craving to know the origin of things and to have a continuity with his past. Set as they were in primordial time, they offered man a world of absolute realities wherein all that man did or intended to do had already been done. Hence, they were paradigmatic — that is, they offered models of human conduct based upon reminders of enduring truths.

Since then, various authors have attempted to write in this vein in an effort to imitate the early myths and achieve similar effects. More modern literary myth-makers have attempted to respond imaginatively to a system of abstractions, or to explore the nature of an idealized world composed along the lines of their particular moral, philosophical, or theological commitments. The line of such creators extends from Plato, whose myths were attempts to clarify philosophical concepts, to such recent authors as J. R. R. Tolkien, whose fantasy world of *The Lord of the Rings* has moral — and cosmic — implications that give it mythic proportions. George MacDonald stands prominently in this line.[13]

When a given story achieved mythic quality, MacDonald was

[13]Referring to modern myth-makers such as Kafka and Novalis, C. S. Lewis writes: "MacDonald is the greatest genius of this kind whom I know" (*Anthology*, p. 16).

fond of referring to it as containing a "central spot of red." Writing to his wife on one occasion, he complained to her of the quality of certain stories he happened to be reading, and explained: "As stories they just want the *one central spot of red* — the wonderful thing which, whether in a fairy story of a word or a human being, is the life and depth — whether of truth or humour or pathos — the eye to the face of it — the thing that shows the unshowable . . ." (*GMDW*, p. 326; italics are Greville's). It is with these "spots of red" in MacDonald's own writings — that is, with their mythic qualities — that we are especially concerned in this present volume, as we consider the separate stories and their themes.

It should be emphasized, therefore, lest any misunderstand, that the fantasies are not merely anecdotes and illustrations of theological ideas; at their best they are imaginative and symbolic explorations of a vision of the significance of life. Although one readily acknowledges that much of MacDonald's work is too overtly didactic, his best imaginative writings are artistic in a high sense of the term. Emotions are not simply described to us; they are created within us. We are made to feel awe in the depths of our beings. The effects that one experiences are those that great myths have always created within man. This is not to say that MacDonald's writings are a sacred revelation, but to suggest that the open-minded reader may well have moments when he feels himself more near the ultimately Real than he has yet been.

To undertake to help the reader understand more fully what a given story is suggesting on the mythic level is presumptuous; criticism always is. Some will feel, I am sure, that I detract from, rather than enhance, what a certain tale has communicated to them. The "unshowable" is often very private in character, and just as often it suffers from discursive exposition. Then, too, a book of this size commenting upon so large a body of work must needs leave much unsaid. To readers who do not know, or share, MacDonald's religious convictions, many episodes in the fantasies may communicate meanings that are quite different from the

Introduction

ones I am seeing, or that MacDonald himself intended. Mac-
Donald would not object to this, as his comment on his fairy
tales reveals: "Everyone ... who feels the story, will read its
meaning after his own nature and development. . . . Your meaning
may be superior to mine."[14] But since he was both a keen
thinker and a thoroughly committed Christian, consciously entertaining the purpose of reading the significance of all of human
experience in Christian terms, and of using his art as a means
of ministering to men, it would seem safe to assume he intended
to project in his symbolic fantasies themes in harmony with his
Christian convictions. It is my intention, therefore, to trace
MacDonald's dominant religious ideas through his works, concentrating upon one main theme for each story. Inasmuch as
almost all his themes are present in any one work, once the
reader has a firm understanding of how a given theme is expressed in one tale, he is better able to discern for himself its
imaginative expression in others.

Good criticism operates upon the faith that what it is able to
accomplish is at best but an aid to the reader's more complete
experience of the primary work itself; it never sees itself as a
substitute for that experience. Therefore, this present work,
though it endeavors to be a self-sufficient piece of criticism, fails
seriously to achieve its purpose whenever it may be used by
someone as a means of "understanding MacDonald's message"
without his reading the imaginative works firsthand. I offer this
exposition because these works, read by themselves alone, may
strike today's reader as too often being recondite and obscure.
But the reader must first have seen for himself, however dimly,
the red spot glowing in the tale as he read it, else he will never
really know the thrill of that encounter.

[14]*ADO*, pp. 316-17.

CHAPTER ONE

"Corage!
God Mend Al!"

" 'All a man has to do,
is to better what he can.' "
—the knight in *Phantastes*

A noticeable tension exists between the above title and epigraph. The title is an anagram, formed from the letters of
George MacDonald's name, which he used as his family motto.
It suggests his strong confidence in the purpose of God ultimately
to overrule all evil and recompense all suffering. But MacDonald
also saw man not as a passive beneficiary of this process, but as
a co-creator, enlisted by God to have a large share in the creative
process whereby good is realized. Both MacDonald's life and his
writings evidence the strength with which he held each of these
convictions, and the success with which he blended them.

George MacDonald was born on December 10, 1824, at Huntly,
in Aberdeenshire, Scotland. The history of the area is rich with
tales of warring clans, treacherous massacres, vicious hatreds, and
deep loyalties. Huntly is a small town situated in a valley, with
the River Bogie running through it, and the ancient Huntly
Castle standing nearby. The people are staunch Celts whose stern
outlook on life was molded, in MacDonald's time, by the hardships arising from both peasant farming and the flax and wool

weaving industries. Religiously, they adhered sternly to John Knox's Calvinism.

MACDONALD'S FATHER

When George MacDonald was eight his mother died of tuberculosis, the same disease that persistently claimed a large number of family members throughout MacDonald's lifetime, including four of his own children. Although the grandmother was nearby and his new stepmother was kindly and compassionate, he looked to his father to be both father and mother to him, and the two established a strong and beautiful realtionship.[1] As a young man MacDonald wrote letters to his father, consulting him on his main decisions and confiding in him his thoughts and opinions — letters which are a rich source of material on MacDonald's personal life and thought. And the father's correspondence reveals him to be worthy of such confidence. Greville, the biographer son to whom we have already alluded, records a great many of these letters.

Greville depicts George MacDonald, Sr., as a man of legendary toughness. He records of his grandfather with pride:

> In 1825 my grandfather's left leg was amputated above the knee for white swelling, as tuberculous disease of the joint was then named, two years previous treatment with blisters and seton having proved unsuccessful. My father was told by the doctor who operated —it being before the days of chloroform —how the patient refused the customary stupefying dose of whisky, or even to have his face covered, preferring to watch the operation; and that only for one moment, when the knife first transfixed the flesh, did he turn his face away and ejaculate a faint, sibilant "whiff!" (GMDW, p. 34)

[1] See Lewis, *Anthology*, pp. 10-11. Woolf, *GK*, pp. 13-15, rejects this view, finding instead repressed rebelliousness and guilt in MacDonald's relationship with his father.

2

"Corage! God Mend All!"

He was indeed of stern fiber. But this side of the man was balanced by his sense of humor and capacity for understanding his family. Family life, according to Greville, was idyllic:

> Sufficient discipline ruled the home. A look of displeasure from the beloved father was punishment for any sin, while his rebuke was awful indeed. Any complaints against their wild escapades, unless involving disobedience, he would smile at, though he might warn and restrict. There was plenty for the hungriest boys of all that was necessary — except, to be sure, oxygen indoors; but clothes were mostly shabby, and the money was always scarce. On the other hand there were cattle in the byre, horses in the stable, wild bees' nests in the stone dykes, whose honeycomb eaten like bread was a priceless joy. . . . (GMDW, p. 54)

The tone here is obviously glowing and probably somewhat disturbing to most contemporary readers, living as we do in an age of debunking realism. It is not our purpose, however — even if it were possible — to try to penetrate this facade simply to arrive at more flesh-and-blood portraiture. The point is that George MacDonald's perception of his father, both in boyhood and in manhood, was a continual source of admiration and delight to him. Our understanding of this relationship helps greatly to explain MacDonald's later ideas about the Fatherhood of God. The wrathful Heavenly Father of some Scottish Calvinists was morally far inferior to the earthly counterpart he knew. Further, the strong yet loving and sympathetic fathers that people MacDonald's fiction, giving unerring spiritual counsel, have his own father as their model.

RELIGIOUS BACKGROUND

The religious convictions of MacDonald's family were strict. His grandmother was famous for her narrow piety: she even committed her son's violin to the flames, lest playing it be detrimental to his faith and that of others. The family was deeply involved

3

in the Evangelical movement that gave birth to the Scottish Free Church in 1843. The issues that prompted the formation of the Free Church, however, had considerably more to do with church government than with doctrine. The Scottish Presbyterianism that ruled in MacDonald's boyhood home maintained essentially the rigid Calvinist doctrines of its founder, John Knox. It was Knox, himself a student of John Calvin, who brought the Reformation to Scotland in the middle of the sixteenth century. His convictions, elaborated in the strongly worded Westminster Confession of the mid-seventeenth century, had narrowed and hardened in the people's minds through centuries of repetition. The resulting system became deeply offensive to MacDonald, and he worked to expose its shortcomings all his life. To understand his own thought better, we must keep in mind the doctrines he was reacting against.

The chief beliefs of Knox's Calvinism are the absolute power, justice, and holiness of God, and the total sinfulness of man. Man's will was corrupted by the Fall in the Garden of Eden, and he can do nothing to contribute to his own salvation. He deserves eternal damnation. But God in mercy chooses some — the Elect — unconditionally to salvation, and, in justice, condemns others to eternal punishment. Christ died as a substitute for the Elect, taking their just punishment upon himself. Calvary therefore gives God legal justification for sparing them. Their faith and consequently their salvation are bestowed upon them arbitrarily, and do not issue from the moral quality of their lives; personal righteousness is an evidence of salvation, not a cause. Much of what MacDonald found offensive in this system, and the shape of his own beliefs, will be indicated in the following chapters. His reactions are rooted in his boyhood experiences, foremost among them being his relationship to his father.

EARLY EDUCATION

Many elements of MacDonald's fiction also have their roots in his boyhood attitudes and experiences. Any listing of such experiences would include his crusading against liquor (MacDonald was at thirteen the first president of the Huntly Juvenile Temperance Society), his fascination for horses, and his love of the sea. Events at school also play a prominent part in his work. The privilege of receiving an education was open to all, the Scottish tradition being one of equality in education. In fact, young George learned his Latin and mathematics sitting beside the sons of "lairds," or landowners. But this privilege was not without its darker side: the atmosphere of Scottish schools was one of strictest discipline, and incorrect recitations were serious offenses. The inhumane Murdoch Malison, the "dominie" (teacher) in one of MacDonald's better novels, *Alec Forbes of Howglen*, was modeled after his first schoolmaster, whose cruel discipline may have been at least in part responsible for the death of George's younger brother, James. But a second schoolmaster, decidedly more humane than the first, took kindly to George, occasionally inviting him to his home before and after school hours. Thus encouraged, MacDonald excelled his fellow pupils and even helped with the teaching. This teacher no doubt furnishes the pattern for the many ideal schoolmasters who live in MacDonald's work.

CONTACT WITH FAERIE

When MacDonald was sixteen he enrolled in Aulton Grammar School in Aberdeen, some forty miles distant, and there he won a "bursary" or university scholarship, which enabled him to enter King's College. His main course of study there was Chemistry and Natural Philosophy (i.e., Physics), but his desire to become a medical doctor was frustrated by lack of money. Having acquired a working knowledge of German, he became increasingly interested in language and literature, and began writing a considerable amount of poetry. He took his M.A. in April of 1845.

The 1842-43 session was a year of delay in his formal studies, made necessary by his poverty, and he may have taken a position which involved cataloguing a neglected library somewhere in

5

northern Scotland.[2] No precise records remain of this experience, but the many scenes in his novels picturing characters making spiritual discoveries and having traumatic experiences in libraries (such as Mr. Cupples in *Alec Forbes* and the narrator in *Lilith*) lead one to suppose that MacDonald himself faced some spiritual crisis at this time. Greville quotes a passage from MacDonald's early novel, *The Portent*, as probably having autobiographical significance:

> *Now I was in my element. . . . The very outside of a book had a charm to me. It was a kind of sacrament —an outward and visible sign of an inward and spiritual grace; as, indeed, what on God's earth is not? . . . I began to nibble at that portion of the collection which belonged to the sixteenth century. . . . I found nothing, to my idea, but love-poems without any love in them, and so I soon became weary. But I found in the library what I liked far better —many romances of a very marvellous sort, and plentiful interruption they gave to the formation of the catalogue. I likewise came upon a whole nest of German classics. . . . Happening to be a tolerable reader of German, I found in these volumes a mine of wealth inexhaustible. (GMDW, p. 73)*

Two elements are to be noted in this passage. First, it presents MacDonald's early conviction that God works on behalf of man through the external world of nature and event. All things in "God's earth" are a "visible sign of an inward and spiritual grace." This developing view suggests a certain departure from a strict

[2]See Muriel Hutton, "The George MacDonald Collection," *Yale University Library Gazette*, 51 (1976), 74-85, for an alternate view. In reading MacDonald's letters contained in the Beinecke Rare Book and Manuscript Library at Yale University, Ms. Hutton finds no evidence to support Greville's undocumented assertion of this experience, and therefore questions it, together with certain other details of Greville's account of his father's life. In interesting contrast is Woolf's fantasizing (*GK*, pp. 16-17) that MacDonald fell in love that summer with a girl of the family who owned the library, and was jilted, causing him psychological pain that he tried repeatedly to assuage imaginatively throughout his novel-writing career.

"Corage! God Mend Al!"

Calvinist one of the nature of God and his presence in the world. MacDonald is beginning to recognize truth as being incarnational rather than strictly propositional. We will explore this conviction of Chapter Three and consider how important it is to our understanding of the world of the fantasies.

Second, the above passage suggests MacDonald's enlarging literary interests. Indeed, certain "German classics" began to affect his imagination profoundly, particularly the great German fairy tales. Among them, two works — E.T.W. Hoffmann's *The Golden Pot* and Novalis's *Heinrich von Ofterdingen* — came to have such compelling effect that a direct comparison of them with such early writings as *Phantastes* becomes a profitable study. These happy contacts greatly supplemented MacDonald's native Scottish love of the land of Faerie, and furnished the basic inspiration for his own magnificent fairy tales, together with many of their themes and their special symbolic character.

Another influence on MacDonald was the general philosophic position of German Romanticism, which afforded him a specific basis for challenging and modifying some of the tenets of his Calvinist theology. The German Romantics were marked by a tendency to contemplate and idealize man, his emotions, and his position in the cosmos.[3] They were convinced that all things are related and that the universe is characterized by a pervading unity, a unity discoverable to man's reason governed by his intuition. They were much concerned that man's reason be viewed in light of his total being rather than allowed to become his controlling faculty, discrediting the imagination and destroying man's spirit. In addition, they had an appreciation for individuality and a conviction that one's life can have an inner harmony commensurate with that which they saw in the outer universe. To them, the most important aspect of man's inner being is his yearning after the eternal and the infinite — a type of spiritual love which draws man toward the divine. This love finds its

[3] A good source to consult for a discussion of the main traits of German Romanticism is Oskar Walzel, *German Romanticism* (New York: Putnam, 1932).

counterpart in the love of man for woman, so that passionate love mirrors spiritual love. Lastly, they were convinced that poetry is absolute reality, ultimate truth, knowledge itself. Such outspoken claims for verbal art are found most specifically in Novalis's thought, with which MacDonald apparently had the strongest affinity. His own claims for the moral and spiritual efficacy of the spirit of poetry and song are remarkably large in such works as *Phantastes* and *At the Back of the North Wind*.

During this break from his university studies, then, MacDonald's imagination was growing and his own religious views were being modified. What begins to emerge is a dynamic synthesis of orthodox Calvinism and German Romanticism.

PORTRAIT OF THE COLLEGE STUDENT

The portrait of MacDonald in his college days is one of a rather dreamy — but on occasions fiery — young Celt. He was a debater, an enthusiast of the then popular parlor game of charades, and a lover of beautiful clothes, being especially fond of his Scottish tartan coat. Somewhat aloof and reserved, he gave the general impression of being a thoughtful youth whose full powers were yet to be realized. Physically he was never strong — he suffered periods throughout his life of bronchitis, asthma, and what may have been tuberculosis. But his active mind was busy seeking a faith that would account more fully for the nature of life as he was experiencing it and as those fascinating German writers saw it to be.

He was writing poetry for his own solace during his college days, and one source of poetic inspiration for him was an attractive and talented cousin, Helen MacKay, some three years his senior. They had been childhood playmates, and they conducted a correspondence in later years, but she was of most help to him at this time, encouraging his literary pursuits. When Greville was collecting data for his book, the aged Helen recalled "a favorite saying of his then was, 'I wis we war a' deid!' and that he often repeated it in after life" (*GMDW*, p. 64). Most likely, this fascination for death should be understood in the light of his strong and rather complex attitudes toward death which we shall note in his writings — especially in *Lilith* — and which were now being shaped by the German Romantics. It does not in itself necessarily argue for a morbid depression of spirit, bitterness, or a rejection of life.[4]

MARRIAGE

Upon leaving King's College, MacDonald took a tutorship in Fulham, a parish in London, and during this period he began to court Louisa Powell, sister-in-law to the now-married Helen MacKay. She was the dutiful but light-hearted daughter of a stern Puritan whose family business was in the leather trade. His experience in teaching having proved rather disappointing, MacDonald now began to prepare for the ministry, a step which he had been contemplating for some time, and entered Highbury Theological College in London in 1848. His university training enabled him to complete the four-year course in two years, and he was soon doing apprentice preaching. Mr. Powell's doubts concerning his prospective son-in-law's suitability for his daughter were thus sufficiently overcome for him to consent to the marriage, and the wedding took place on March 8, 1851. The couple settled at Arundel, in West Sussex, where MacDonald had his first charge as pastor of the Trinity Congregational Church.

THE HETERODOX PASTOR

The new pastor at Arundel was already well on the road to forming beliefs which rendered him no longer acceptable to

[4]Woolf accepts MacDonald's use of this expression as certain evidence that he was "deeply mournful and depressed" during this period (*GK*, p. 17). That he was pre-occupied with death is also evident from the poem "Love Me, Beloved," which he presented to his wife on their wedding day, and which Woolf quotes in support of his contention (*GK*, pp. 20-22). Still, these somber expressions do not prove that MacDonald was mentally unhealthy. His fascination for death, with the expectation of ecstatic experience beyond, was more probably being fed by Novalis's attitudes on the subject, found throughout his writings.

Nonconformist congregations, and his experience with the inflexible attitudes of the lay people there soon strengthened him in his convictions. MacDonald's beliefs, rooted in his childhood experiences, had grown steadily during the 1840's. We can note at this point, therefore, the general directions his thinking was taking.

MacDonald writes in his novel *Weighed and Wanting* many years later: "I well remember . . . feeling as a child that I did not care for God to love me if he did not love everybody: the kind of love I needed was the love that all men needed, the love that belonged to their nature as the children of the Father, a love he could not give me except he gave it to all men." This passage suggests that as a boy he must have been at least uneasy about the doctrines of limited atonement and unconditional election. With a disposition that could not long maintain a negative approach, he began to feel that God was, as Creator, everyone's Father, and that His mercy extended impartially to all. Excerpts from two letters that Greville provides from the period of his father's tutorship show his state of mind prior to his pastorship:

MacDonald to his Father

One of my greatest difficulties in consenting to think of religion was that I thought I should have to give up my beautiful things and my love for the things God had made. But I find that the happiness springing from all things not in themselves sinful is much increased by religion. God is the God of the beautiful, Religion the love of the Beautiful, and Heaven the home of the Beautiful, Nature is tenfold brighter in the sun of Righteousness, and my love of Nature is more intense since I became a Christian —if indeed I am one. God has not given me such things and forbidden me to enjoy them. . . .

MacDonald to his Uncle

I called on Dr. Adams, but had again the misfortune to find that he was out. I do not think I am right to use the word misfortune, *for the conviction is, I think, growing on me that the smallest events are ordered for us, while yet in perfect consistency with the ordinary course of cause and effect in the world. I am strongly inclined to think that whatever has a moral effect of any kind on our minds, God manages for us. . . . (GMDW, pp. 108-109)*

One quickly notes how some of his most deeply held convictions are emerging. God is the joyous Creator of a beautiful world, and He intends for man to enjoy it. God is behind not only the good and the beautiful in the world, but the so-called "misfortunes" as well, creating an ultimate good for all His children.

Similarly positive are MacDonald's letters to his fiancée, which go beyond mere lover's rhetoric in considering the nature of love, linking it with the life of God:

Is love a beautiful thing, dearest? You and I love: but who created love? Let us ask him to purify our love to make it stronger and more real and more self-denying. I want to love you for ever —so that, though there is not marrying or giving in marriage in heaven, we may see each other there as the best beloved. Oh Louisa, is it not true that our life here is a growing unto life, and our death a being born —our true birth? If there is anything beautiful in this our dreamy life, shall it not shine forth in glory in the bright waking consciousness of heaven? . . . But . . . we can only expect to be a blessing to each other —by doing that which is right. . . . (GMDW, p. 117)

This sentiment is typical of MacDonald's idealization of woman and of the love relationship, an idea we will encounter often in the fantasies. Love of woman, a fuller experience of what love is, becomes a means of loving God better.[5] In addition, the idea here expressed of the possibility of the soul's constant growth, so that it is ever becoming something that it is only tending

---

[5]Cf. MacDonald's discussion of love in his essay "Individual Development," *ADO*, pp. 43-76.

toward now, is destined to become one of his central ideas. This growth is possible only through an active obedience.

Also noteworthy is the tone of each of the above letters. It is not that of an easy sentimentality, as the more casual reader may conclude. Rather, it is a genuine sensitivity to other people, to human experience in general, and to God. It comes to MacDonald's aid frequently in his writings, helping him discern and explain fine ideas and delicate truths that a coarser sensibility would miss utterly.

These ideas, however, as acceptable as they may be to us today, were far out of keeping with what his Nonconformist parishioners then wanted to hear. Further, when their pastor in 1851 published his translations, "Twelve of the Spiritual Songs of Novalis," they gave him a damning label: he was tainted with German thought.[6] When MacDonald expressed from the pulpit his hope that animals would have a share in the joys of heaven, and that the opportunity for the heathen to be saved did not end at their death, the congregation was aroused to indignant action. They drastically reduced his salary in the hope he would thereby be forced to resign. Never reluctant to accept poverty if such were God's will, MacDonald simply responded that he and his family would live on less. But when he saw that his staying was encouraging a schism, he resigned in 1853.

FREE-LANCE PREACHER AND LECTURER

A period of great hardship and disappointment followed. Poverty-stricken, MacDonald took his family to the industrial metropolis of Manchester and rented a room on Renshaw Street, preaching regularly for those who would listen, and expressing freely his growing convictions. He was especially attracted to Manchester because of the presence there of Alexander John Scott, Principal of Owens College, whom he greatly admired,

---

[6]". . . he was emboldened to print in Arundel his translations . . . for private circulation as a Christmas gift to his friends" (*GMDW*, p. 159).

and to whom he later dedicated his novel *Robert Falconer*. He succeeded in drawing a certain following of intellectuals, to whom he began lecturing on English literature and physical science as well as theology.

But he was constantly dependent upon the dole of his few admirers, while fighting tuberculosis and attacks of bronchitis, and trying to strengthen the scant sympathies of family members, both Powells and MacDonalds.[7] It is to his father's credit that he tried to be sympathetic to his son during this period, though he advised him in one letter to "give over the fruitless game of poetry, and apply yourself to the preaching of the Gospel." MacDonald's sorrow was deepened by two deaths in his family: his brother John died of tuberculosis in 1858, and his father died suddenly a month later. His father's death was a particularly great blow to him, for there had been not only a constant correspondence between father and son but also an unusually deep emotional bond.

THE YOUNG FATHER

Greville, however, indicates that as a father MacDonald did not profit as much from his father's reputed example as he might have. In spite of the adulatory tone that Greville maintains throughout his biography, in his later *Reminiscences of a Specialist* he depicts a somewhat more human father. For instance, he remarks, ". . . my father, I think, did not altogether understand

---

[7]Greville gives this picture of family conditions at his birth: "When at last I arrived on a foggy winter's day in 1856, my father, then lying at the house of his friend, Alexander J. Scott, Principal of Owens College, Manchester, seemed to be dying of haemorrhage from the lungs. Yet in spite of scribbling forbidden notes to my mother to reciprocate her joy that a boy was now added to their three little girls, the danger was arrested. Within a fortnight my mother was preparing to leave a city that offered small chance of his cure. For two years he had by teaching subsisted precariously, heroic alike in industry and ailing, while my mother tended and taught her children, superinteeeeen kept the house and its furniture spotless, yet always the lover and support of her husband . . ." (*ROS*, pp. 12, 13). Greville's praise of his mother is consistently strong.

children, though in his books he so fully realized their needs,"
and he records the following:

> When I was nine, my father gave me a box of tools, and a little
> bench with an adorable vice that squeaked vilely but never held. They
> gave me infinite happiness. . . . One recompense was an admonishment
> from my father over an attempt at box-making; and I have never
> forgotten it: "If ever you do anything badly and content yourself with
> saying, 'Oh, that'll have to do!' then you may be sure it won't do
> at all!" It represented well a stoic quality in his own creed: "God,"
> he once said, "is not hard to please, but it is impossible to satisfy
> Him". . . . My father began to teach me Latin when I was nine, I
> think. The initial lesson dealt with the opening lines of the Aeneid.
> He first translated them, and tried to make me feel their metric thrill;
> then I had to commit them to my impossible memory. But I did not
> understand him; and the words had no more meaning than if he had
> himself invented them just for a lesson. Such a system might be good
> for a clever boy; but it was worse than useless for me. For it suggested
> that foreign words were hateful and meant only tasks. He failed almost
> as much with Euclid. I recall his patient attempts to explain, with the
> help of matches, the first of the Axioms; and how, hypnotized by my
> own wrong version, even punishment failed to help me. At last the
> pons asinorum, easily traversed by a sister, proved me hopeless. And
> there the lessons ceased. Yet later at school I was singularly facile with
> geometry. [8]

MacDonald was his own stern taskmaster, and evidently this
stern attitude, coupled with high expectations for both intellectual endeavor and moral conduct, shaped his family life as well
as his writings. On the one hand, he held a vision of mercy and
patience of widest compass; on the other, he felt intensely that
men were responsible to follow goodness with dedication of
spirit and to be diligent in realizing their highest ethical and

[8]ROS, pp. 15, 31.

intellectual potential. In retrospect, Greville apparently entertains some reservations about the behavior these convictions produced.

EARLY WRITINGS

The brighter side of the 1850's is that they mark the beginning of MacDonald's career as a writer. In addition to sustaining throughout his life steady preaching engagements and regular lecture tours, he produced, with amazing energy, over fifty published volumes of fantasy, poetry, novels, fairy tales and young people's stories, sermons, essays, translations of German authors, and literary criticism. In this study we are concerned primarily with his fantasies, but it is important to our understanding of MacDonald to consider his career as a poet and novelist as well.

MacDonald's initial success came in 1855 with the publication of *Within and Without*, an extended dramatic poem that melo-dramatically details the experiences of an aspiring monk who escapes the monastery, marries, and comes through many difficult experiences into a true relation with God. This was followed in 1857 by a second small volume of poems, the most noted of which is "The Hidden Life."[9] He discovered his true literary strength in 1858, however, with *Phantastes: A Faerie Romance for Men and Women*. It is a fantasy in which MacDonald presents the hero as discovering moral and spiritual truths in a rapidly occurring series of highly symbolic adventures in Faerie. In the chapters that follow we will find this symbolism a rich source of illustration of MacDonald's thought.

MacDonald was disturbed with a certain reviewer's attempt to call *Phantastes* allegory, insisting that if a reader find some truths behind its symbolism, well and good, but it was to be

[9]Reis takes a dim view of the quality of MacDonald's poetry (cf. pp. 23-26), and Woolf manages only faint praise (*GK*, p. 39). For a more thorough and sympathetic treatment, see Glenn Edward Sadler, "Cosmic Vision: A Study of the Poetry of George MacDonald," Diss. Aberdeen University 1966.

read simply for the joy of the story. The story exhibits the author's ability, found as well in the later children's fairy tales and *Lilith*, to invest the fairy world with a startling reality while at the same time retaining its atmosphere of magic and wonder.

LITERARY FRIENDS AND INFLUENCES

MacDonald's budding writing career enabled him to become acquainted with many prominent Victorian authors, but he became intimate with few. Among the most interesting of his close friendships was one with Lady Byron, the poet's widow, who admired MacDonald so profoundly that from 1855 until her death in 1860 she became the MacDonald family's steady benefactor.[10] Because of his poor health, she sponsored the family for a winter in Algiers in 1856-57, and in her will she left them 300 pounds. It was at her home that Henry Crabb Robinson, the famous diarist, met MacDonald in April of 1859. He describes MacDonald as "a very interesting man . . . an invalid and a German scholar. . . . His connections are among the Dissenters . . . yet [he] is quite liberal."[11] Lady Byron was as well responsible for introducing MacDonald to several others in the literary circles of the time, and he then became intimately acquainted with Frederick Denison Maurice, Charles Kingsley, Matthew Arnold, and John Ruskin.

Nevertheless, very little information exists on the exact nature of these friendships. Greville writes: "My father and mother, what with his ill-health and the demands of the young family upon herself, together with their poverty, could not move much in the social world. Yet . . . Charles Kingsley, Matthew Arnold, and Henry Crabb Robinson ranked among their intimates, even

[10]This patronage gives interesting insight into Lady Byron's character: MacDonald stood considerably nearer her ideal than did her late husband. She is fictionalized as Lady Bernard in *The Vicar's Daughter* — a most flattering portrait.

[11]Edith J. Morley, ed., *Henry Crabb Robinson on Books and Their Writers*, 11 (London: Dent, 1938), 783. A friend of a large number of nineteenth-century authors, Robinson left much information about them in his diary and his correspondence.

if they did not meet very often ..." (*GMDW*, p. 300). One gets
the feeling that the MacDonalds were on the periphery of the
social life of their time, maintaining certain warm ties with those
who admired MacDonald's thought and abilities, but simply plac-
ing higher value on such things as family life and MacDonald's
ministry rather than on social activity as such. Those friends who
were closest to them are described by Greville as being almost
a part of the MacDonald family. Perhaps the closest family friend
was Charles L. Dodgson (Lewis Carroll), who, Greville writes,
was "especially intimate in our home, as in our hearts" (*GMDW*,
p. 301). He calls him "Uncle Dodgson," and recalls how the
manuscript of *Alice in Wonderland* was first submitted to Mac-
Donald for his evaluation ("illustrated with pen-and-ink sketches
and minutely penned in printing characters" (*GMDW* p. 342).
MacDonald suggested it be read to his children for their reactions, and as a result of their lively enthusiasm, it was published.
This closeness is understandable, because the two men shared
a love of children and an especial ability to recreate imaginatively
a children's world.

With two of the more prominent literati listed above, Arnold
and Ruskin, MacDonald shared a vivid sense of moral urgency.
Although both stand rather far from MacDonald's religious commitment, MacDonald consistently placed the necessity of adher-
ing to high moral concepts above any sectarian agreement on the
dogmatic doctrinal basis for these concepts, and, unlike most
Evangelicals, he could find an enriching fellowship with men of
differing doctrinal persuasions. He did share common ground
with both men: Arnold celebrated Wordsworth, whom Mac-
Donald greatly admired for, among other qualities, the strength
of his moral vision and his application of moral ideas to life, and
Ruskin built a careful argument for a moral aesthetic.[12] In addition, MacDonald acted as a confidante to Ruskin during his

[12]See Arnold's poem "Memorial Verses" for his general tribute and his
article on Wordsworth for his specific emphasis upon Wordsworth's morality; see MacDonald's essay "Wordsworth's Poetry," *ADO*, pp. 245-263, for
his assessment of Wordsworth. Ruskin oulines his moral aesthetic in *Modern Painters*.

tumultuous love affair with Rose La Touche, an episode about which Greville includes much interesting material (*GMDW*, pp. 328 ff.).

The friends who did most to influence the direction of MacDonald's theological thinking during this time were Alexander John Scott and Frederick Denison Maurice. Little can be said about the precise religious position of Scott, since he left no important writings. His orthodoxy had also been questioned — he was disfranchised from the Presbyterian ministry for preaching universalism — and thus he was able to encourage and counsel sympathetically the rejected minister from Arundel at the crucial time of his moving to Manchester. But the most prominent Victorian theologian to influence MacDonald's thought was Maurice. He was an ambivalent figure who, like MacDonald, tended to be too liberal for the conservatives and too conservative for the liberals. He was ahead of his time, a High Churchman with a social conscience — he coined the phrase "Christian Socialism" and was the leader of that movement in the 1840's. Throughout his career as educator and minister he published widely. He was a Trinitarian, but his spirit was more Unitarian than Evangelical. Most Evangelical formulations of doctrine appeared too crass and materialistic to him, and he repeatedly attempted a more profoundly spiritual interpretation of the biblical "proof texts" used by Evangelicals to establish these positions. A man whose deep practical spirituality lent a moral beauty to his life which was widely admired, Maurice was ecumenical in spirit, feeling that there was some truth in all religious experience, Christian and otherwise.

MacDonald became a disciple of his in the late 1850's. Among the ideas that MacDonald clearly shared with him were his stress upon the Fatherhood of God and the conviction that Christ is absolutely at one with the Father (a doctrine that renders impossible any view of the Atonement as bringing about a change in God's attitude toward man — forgiveness was God's disposition from eternity past). Both rejected the idea that sin would be eternally punished, emphasized the "Inner Light" with the possibility of revelation to the individual apart from Scripture (but not inharmonious with it), and insisted that theology undergirds all of life, all branches of knowledge being subservient to it.

Within the Christian Socialist movement being shaped by Maurice, Charles Kingsley was a prominent novelist. Although MacDonald was not actively a part of this movement, he shared Kingsley's concern for the social and religious problems of the laboring people.[13] MacDonald's novels *Robert Falconer* and *Guild Court* manifest this type of social concern. *The Water Babies*, Kingsley's moralizing fairy story published in 1863, also bears a resemblance, perhaps derivative, to MacDonald's *Phantastes* (1858).

THE TURN TO THE NOVEL

The popular success of such propagandistic novelists as Kingsley may have been a factor in MacDonald's turning to the writing of novels. No doubt another factor was that *Phantastes* was not widely praised by the public or by critics. MacDonald must have been disappointed with the public's inability to interpret his message with satisfying accuracy when it was couched in symbols.

Greville notes from a study of the letters of the early sixties his father's increasing "conviction that the world was so sorely in need of his message" (*GMDW*, p. 324). Then, too, although MacDonald seems to have been singularly free of desire to make money, his family needed to eat, and he knew it would help if his pen could be made to pay. His publisher friend George Murray Smith urged him: ". . . if you would but write novels, you would find all the publishers saving up to buy them of you! Nothing but fiction pays" (*GMDW*, p. 318). The result was that

[13]Joseph Ellis Baker, *The Novel and the Oxford Movement* (Princeton: Princeton University Press, 1932). Though old, this is a useful study of how the novel was at this time used for religious purposes. Baker discusses a number of minor religious novelists. So also does Robert Lee Woolf in *Gains and Losses: Novels of Faith and Doubt in Victorian England* (New York: Garland, 1977). Woolf is good for plot summaries.

he turned from fantasy to the novel in order to communicate his convictions to the world.

MacDonald possessed the unmistakable gift of telling a story with compelling power and narrative grace, and he understood clearly the art of novel writing. Nevertheless, his early attempts at novels were too weighted with preaching for any publisher to accept.[14] Then a remarkable exception, *The Portent*, appeared in *Cornhill Magazine*, summer issue, in 1860. This short novel is interestingly free from direct teaching; its plot turns upon the fact that some of the characters possess Celtic second sight. When his wife pressed him for its meaning, MacDonald somewhat embarrassedly confessed that he simply "wrote it for the tale" (*GMDW*, p. 318).

In his dedicatory preface to *The Portent*, MacDonald observes that a novel must offer insight into human nature and experience, and it must do so in a form characterized by a "harmony within," or inner consistency. These simple but telling artistic standards go far in measuring the art of MacDonald's subsequent novels, their strengths and weaknesses.

His first published novel was *David Elginbrod* (1863), which, although it somewhat relieved his financial distress, contained sufficient heterodoxy to prevent him from receiving the Chair of Rhetoric and Belles Lettres at Edinburgh University for which he applied in 1865. The kernel idea for the story came to MacDonald at a business dinner of literary celebrities to which he was invited. He was deeply affected by hearing a journalist recite an old Scotch epitaph:

Here lie I, Martin Elginbrodde;
Hae mercy o' my soul, Lord God;
As I wad do, were I Lord God,
An' ye war Martin Elginbrodde!

[14] After publishing *Phantastes*, MacDonald wrote a play entitled *If I Had a Father*, which he then turned into a novel entitled *Seekers and Finders*. He failed to secure a publisher for the novel, and finally published the play with some fairy stories in *The Gifts of the Christ Child and Other Tales* in 1882.

"Corage! God Mend Al!"

This verse must have suggested to MacDonald man's need for God's mercy, and the essential unity between the divine and the human, ideas which are important in all his writings. *David Elginbrod*, whose hero is modeled after MacDonald's father, was flatteringly received by the critics, and met with moderate success. It was even translated into German in 1873.

MacDonald, however, apparently was not entirely satisfied with the prospect of writing only realistic novels. He wanted to try again to make his readers understand symbolic tales. The following year, 1864, marks the appearance of *Adela Cathcart*, a work that attempts to bring together fantasy and realism. In it a framework of realistic narrative contains a number of experiments in symbolic tales, from fairy story through various moral anecdotes to parable. But the experiment was not well received, which evidently made MacDonald determined to keep the two genres more distinctly separate. His own dissatisfaction is registered in the thorough reworking that he gave the material for a second edition in 1882, omitting from it three of his better stories — "The Light Princess," "The Shadows," and "The Giant's Heart" — and reprinting them elsewhere as children's stories.

Reverting to realism, he produced in the following two years two ambitious novels, *Alec Forbes of Howglen* and *Annals of a Quiet Neighbourhood*. The former is a remarkably vivid tale of an orphan girl and Alec Forbes, which traces their growing up together, both physically and spiritually, and their eventual love. The latter book, narrated by a young pastor, depicts his experiences in a small-town parish — experiences based upon MacDonald's life in Arundel. His name now established as an important young novelist, MacDonald began to rapidly produce novels which expressed his interpretation of life. They fall into two general categories, the Scottish and the English. The first of the former is *David Elginbrod*, with its initial Scottish setting and its studied attempt to reproduce the Scottish dialect; the second is *Alec Forbes of Howglen*. In the category of English novels, the first is *Adela Cathcart*, with its framework of thoroughly English setting and customs, and *Annals of a Quiet Neighbourhood* is, if *The Portent* is discounted, the second.

Over the next thirty years he produced more than twenty novels, in addition to the above titles, that blend realism and romance. The works can be divided into the two ethnic categories defined (though there is, of course, some overlapping). In the English group, chronologically, fall the following titles: *Guild Court* (1868), *The Seaboard Parish* (1868), *The Vicar's Daughter* (1872), *Wilfrid Cumbermede* (1872), *Thomas Wingfold, Curate* (1876), *Paul Faber, Surgeon* (1879), *Mary Marston* (1881), *Weighed and Wanting* (1882), *What's Mine's Mine* (1886), *Home Again* (1887), and *There and Back* (1891). The remaining titles in the Scottish group are *Robert Falconer* (1868), *Malcolm* (1875), *The Marquis of Lossie* (1877), *Sir Gibbie* (1879), *Warlock O'Glenwarlock* (1882), *Donal Grant* (1883), *The Elect Lady* (1888), *A Rough Shaking* (1890), *The Flight of the Shadow* (1891), *Heather and Snow* (1893), and *Salted with Fire* (1897). One historical novel, *St. George and St. Michael* (1876), set during the Puritan Revolution, is particularly interesting for its sympathetic treatment of the English Catholics.

Viewing all the novels as a body, one notes little change either in technique or in underlying ideas. A few of his works, such as *The Elect Lady* and *The Flight of the Shadow*, are obviously too quickly written and of inferior quality. It is also true that one finds stock incidents and characters in all of the novels. Nevertheless, MacDonald's love of life and his psychological insights, together with his keen ability to reproduce Scottish dialect and the flavor of Scottish attitudes, result in many delightful portions, particularly in the Scottish group. And his epigrammatic turn of phrase coupled with his exacting insights into experience often gives memorable expression to basic moral and spiritual ideas, many of which could hardly be denied, even by the most unsympathetic reader.

CHILDREN'S LITERATURE

Nor is this all. MacDonald also stands as one of the century's finest authors of children's literature. In 1869 he accepted the

22

editorship of a periodical for children entitled *Good Words for the Young*. It lasted for only four years; in fact, MacDonald edited the final two years' copies without pay. He was fortunate to have some of his own fairy stories first published in it, although the ill feelings of those whose manuscripts were refused made him determine that he would do no more editing at any salary. But his love of the children's story and fairy tale continued throughout his lifetime, and most of his titles are still found in the children's rooms of public libraries. His fairy tales were published separately on various occasions, and have appeared in many different editions down to the present time.

Among his children's books the most widely read are *At the Back of the North Wind* (1871), *The Princess and the Goblin* (1872), and *The Princess and Curdie* (1883), each of which contains genuine charm. (Later we will find them to contain skillfully wrought representations of some of his main ideas.) MacDonald's great strength in each is the manner in which he makes the supernatural seem immediately real. Two full-length novels, *Ranald Bannerman's Boyhood* (1871) and *Gutta Percha Willie: The Working Genius* (1873), fall somewhere between the children's stories and the adult fiction, and may most properly be classified as adolescent novels.

LECTURES AND FAMILY AFFAIRS

In addition to his ambitious career as a writer, MacDonald found time for other noteworthy concerns. For a time he was a lecturer at evening classes at King's College, London. (His own university conferred upon him the degree of Doctor of Laws in 1868.) He spent the winter of 1872-73 on a lecture tour of America, in which he visited cities throughout the East and went as far west as St. Louis.[15] As a platform speaker he was very well received, his lectures on Robert Burns being the most popular. During the

[15]See Greville, *ROS*, pp. 47-52, for his glowing account of MacDonald's reception in America.

tour he met the literary great, among them the poet John Green-leaf Whittier and, remarkably, Mark Twain, who later returned the visit to England.

MacDonald's private life was also full. Problems of health prompted his decision to have the family winter regularly in Italy, and in 1891 he planned and built his own home in Bor-dighera, naming it Casa Coraggio, a place large enough for his eleven children. The oldest daughter, Lilia, possessed an extraor-dinary talent for acting, and, although her parents would not allow her to become an actress on the secular stage, for years the family project for each summer was to return to England as a family acting troupe, presenting dramas in public halls and private homes. In their repertoire were *Macbeth*, a version of Zola's *L'Assommoir*, some of Dickens, and many of MacDonald's fairy tales. (The adaptations of the texts for the stage were largely the work of Louisa, MacDonald's wife.) Their most popular pre-sentation was a rendition of *Pilgrim's Progress*; Lilia became quite well-known as Christiana, and MacDonald himself played Mr. Greatheart, the other parts being carried by the other members of the family. On Sunday and Wednesday afternoons Casa Cor-aggio was open to the public, and MacDonald regularly presented devotional discourses and lectures on Dante and on English lit-erature, focusing particularly on Shakespeare.

The activities of these later years, however, were marred by increasing problems of health and the toll of tuberculosis upon the family. Tuberculosis claimed MacDonald's daughter Mary Jo-sephine, engaged to a promising young artist, in 1878; a delicate-natured son in 1879; a recently married daughter in 1884; and the highly talented Lilia in 1891. These heartaches put strong demands upon the solace that his anagram — "Corage! God Mend Al!" — offered.

One noteworthy literary result of the severe trials of Mac-Donald's life is *A Book of Strife, in the Form of the Diary of an Old Soul* (1880), a devotional poem of 366 stanzas, one for each day of the year (including the "extra" day of a leap year). John Ruskin described it as "quaint, full of devotion, high in tone, the best example of the survival of faith in this sceptical age" (*GMDW*, p. 497). Its sentiments are at times strongly mystical and esoteric; nevertheless, MacDonald's sensitive and intimate presentation of the devout soul's various feelings before God are, it seems to me, as fine as any such expressions in English poetry.

MacDonald expressed his convictions in expository form in *The Miracles of our Lord* (1870), three volumes entitled *Unspoken Sermons* (1867, 1886, and 1889), and *The Hope of the Gospel* (1892).[16] He distrusted all abstract systems of thought, and he avoided systematizing his own, but his convictions are thoroughly consistent with each other, and quite comprehensive theologically. He is sensitive to the shortcomings of language and metaphor in presenting divine realities, and he tends to see all doctrinal formulations as being but sets of opinions. But he has, on the other hand, an intense reverence for the text of Scripture, and he speaks compellingly out of careful and profound meditations upon selected Scripture passages, frequently showing a deft ability to handle the Greek text. He is insistent upon the necessity of Christians thinking carefully and consistently upon all of Scripture, and he does not avoid texts that on the surface would appear to negate some of his own positions — for instance, his sermon "It Shall Not Be Forgiven" is based upon Luke 12:10. He does not hesitate to show his righteous indignation toward what he perceived to be the spiritual crassness and intellectual shortsightedness of many in the Christian community of his day. Invariably, his emphasis falls upon the vital importance of a childlike obedience to Scriptural precepts. All those who are interested in his thought should directly consult these sermons and theological essays.

[16]*The Miracles of our Lord* (Wheaton, Ill.: Harold Shaw, 1980). I have edited and published condensations of these sermons: *Creation in Christ* (Wheaton, Ill.: Harold Shaw, 1976), and *Life Essential: The Hope of the Gospel* (Wheaton, Ill.: Harold Shaw, 1974). References to individual sermons will hereafter be by their titles, together with the following abbreviations: *US* I (London, 1867); *US* II (London, 1886); *US* III (London, 1889); and *HG* for *The Hope of the Gospel* (London, 1892).

25

MacDonald's full and varied career came to its close in the 1890's. As an aged man, he aspired to compose a final, crowning fictional statement of his body of convictions, and the result was a second fantasy for adults, entitled *Lilith* (1895). The penetrating logic of its controlling ideas and the haunting reality of its dream imagery make it an outstanding moral fantasy, worthy of careful reading. He died at Ashtead, Surrey, on September 18, 1905; his body was cremated, and his ashes buried at Bordighera.

CONCLUSION

Thus George MacDonald was a writer who articulated his personal vision during the victorian period. He earnestly tried to humanize his Calvinist theological inheritance, both directly, through theological essays, and indirectly, through novels, fantasies, and children's fairy tales. On both the theological and literary scenes, he stood somewhat apart from his contemporaries, quietly learning from many, but with characteristic humility engaging none in controversy and having little to say openly about any of them. He was primarily a poet and novelist, not a controversialist. Interested as he was in penetrating to the truths that lie at the very core of human experience, he aroused few men to oppose him. The extent to which MacDonald succeeded in being a significant force in directing Victorian religious thinking is very difficult to ascertain, but his influence among common people who bought his works must have been considerable.[17]

[17]Judging from the number of editions which most of his works merited — Bulloch in his bibliography commonly lists from ten to twelve for the main novels, and this in England alone — MacDonald's reading public must have been enormous. In addition, Bulloch speaks about his "immense vogue in America," where the pirating of MacDonald's books was so extensive that he gave up the task of listing American editions. (See discussion, Bulloch, pp. 679-86.) The problem of measuring MacDonald's influence is compounded by the fact that he actively eschewed outward success and "worldly" position throughout his life, caring only that he have sufficient money to meet his family's needs. This attitude resulted in the powers of the world neglecting him, except insofar as they could exploit his material for their own profit. (See *GMDW*, pp. 364 and 531, for evidences of this attitude.)

"Corage! God Mend All!"

MacDonald was not a thinker concerned only with internal matters in Evangelicalism, unaware or unheeding of the great issues that confronted the church in his day. He deplored the encroachments of the mechanistic approach of science upon any of the sundry aspects of life. He hated any expression of materialism as well, and treated with keen irony anyone who felt that money was the answer to one's ills. Certainly he did not think that money should be despised, but rather that it should be viewed as sacred — a means to possible good, although not nearly so much good as some people suppose. But the tendency of the period to associate material progress with spiritual values, looking upon riches as a proper reward for work combined with the proper virtues, was to him contemptible.

On the other hand, he was undisturbed by certain contemporary ideas that influenced some other authors to alter greatly or reject completely their orthodox Christian heritage. The rise of evolutionary theory, which many Evangelicals saw as devastating to their faith, was something MacDonald welcomed. Like Robert Browning, he saw it as lending strong support to his doctrine of individual spiritual development and growth, and it reinforced his optimism for the moral future of mankind. Another source of attack on Christian faith, German Higher Criticism of the biblical text, left many intellectuals of the period spiritually bereft, but it disturbed MacDonald little. He was not perturbed chiefly because he felt the raw intellect simply was unable to comprehend Christianity apart from the response of full obedience, and because he exalted the Living Word above the written word. He has little to say about Higher Criticism in his writings, but an essay in *Orts* on Browning's "Christmas Eve" shows his full agreement with that poet's ironic handling of the Gottingen professor who epitomizes for Browning the German rationalist approach to Christianity. The nineteenth-century movements toward social reform receive his full sympathy, apparent in his books like *Robert Falconer*, in which the selfless hero helps the poor slum dwellers.

One must observe, however, that MacDonald's theology stops appreciably short of nineteenth-century liberalism. He had a

strong vision of personal evil and the necessity of purgation from it, and hence had a clear vision of the consuming fires of God's holiness. The righteousness he championed differs from that of the liberal in that he insisted it is not self-generated; it is produced rather by the presence of Christ within the believer. Nor does it earn salvation, being a product of God's indwelling energies. And his emphasis upon subjective experience was not at the expense of the objective reality of God. To MacDonald, man is subsumed in that reality; to the liberal, God is subsumed within the ego. MacDonald's doctrines of the subjugation of the self and of personal immortality also make him distinct from his liberal friends.

MacDonald's convictions have, then, abundant expression in various literary types: sermons, poems, novels, and fantasies. Our study will focus greatest attention upon the fantasies and fairy tales for two reasons: first, because his achievement reaches its highest level in this mythopoeic art; and second, because the not infrequent obscurity of the fantasies can be diminished by carefully noting what specific convictions give form to symbolic incidents and events. Since we are primarily concerned with the way in which his ideas shape his art, it is good to begin by exploring the fantasies for young people. In *The Princess and the Goblin* and *The Princess and Curdie*, one of the most basic tenets of his faith — that salvation is in its very nature the experience of becoming righteous — gives shape to many of the incidents.

Building (upper left) in Huntly, Aberdeenshire, where George MacDonald was born on December 10, 1824.

The Farm, now called Greenkirtle, on the edge of Huntly, where Mac-Donald's parents moved in 1826, and where MacDonald was raised.

The ruins of Huntly Castle, which captured MacDonald's imagination when he was a child.

Aulton Grammar School, Aberdeen, where in 1840 MacDonald was coached in Latin before he entered King's College.

The chapel, King's College, Aberdeen. MacDonald enrolled here in 1840, and graduated in 1845.

Tarrant Street, Arundel, near the lodgings of the newly married MacDonalds.

The Arundel United Reformed Church (formerly the Trinity Congregational Church), where MacDonald was the minister from 1850-1853.

Page dated 1853 in the church account book, showing the entry (third line from top of page) "By ½ yrs. Salary to Rev. G. MacDonald £56.16.0," an appreciable reduction of his former salary of £150 per year.

MacDonald in 1862, about the time he began his novel-writing career.

MacDonald at the height
of his long career.

Louisa Powell MacDonald in 1885.

The complete MacDonald family in 1876, together with prospective son-in-
law E. R. Hughes. Mary Josephine, his fiancée, died of tuberculosis during
their engagement.

Casa Coraggio, the home that MacDonald planned and built at Bordighera, Italy, in 1877, using funds largely donated by friends.

The Brander Library in Huntly, which houses a modest collection of MacDonald's manuscripts and letters.

MacDonald dressed for the role of Mr. Greatheart in the family's dramatic production of Pilgrim's Progress.

CHAPTER TWO

Glowing, Flaming Roses, Red and White

"I was doing the wrong of never
wanting or trying to be better."
—Curdie in *The Princess and Curdie*

In one of the initial meetings between the mystical old queen Irene and Curdie in *The Princess and Curdie*, the queen explains to him about spiritual growth and retrogression:

"... Have you ever heard what some philosophers say —that men were all animals once?"

"No, ma'am."

"It is of no consequence. But there is another thing that is of the greatest consequence —this: that all men, if they do not take care, go down hill to the animals' country; that many men are actually, all their lives, going to be beasts. People knew it once, but it is long since they forgot it."

"I am not surprised to hear it, ma'am, when I think of some of our miners."

"Ah! But you must beware, Curdie, how you say of this man or that man that he is travelling beastward. There are not nearly so many going that way as at first sight you might think. When you met your father on the hill tonight, you stood and spoke together on the same *spot; and although one of you was going up and the other coming down, at a little distance no one could have told which was bound in the one direction and which in the other. Just so two people may be at the same spot in manners and behavior, and yet one may be getting better and the other worse, which is just the greatest of all differences that could possibly exist between them."*

Here is the heart of a concept that appears in almost all of MacDonald's stories. For want of a better term, we may call it his doctrine of becoming.[1] Much of the symbolism of *The Princess and the Goblin* and *The Princess and Curdie* gives imaginative expression to this idea.

MacDonald felt deeply that the great possibility for mankind is to grow into complete godlikeness, so that men shall be one with God. This does not mean that men shall be absorbed into God, as more pantheistic systems hold; rather, as men mature into moral and spiritual perfection, they develop at the same time a more distinct individuality. When men shall become full sons of God, each one willing the right and doing the good as naturally as God Himself does, then they will participate in the blessed fellowship that has always existed between God the Father and Christ the Son. MacDonald's vision is one of an innumerable multitude of redeemed individuals with a final unity of will and spirit.

The work of God toward this great end progresses as slowly

[1]Woolf speaks of MacDonald's "concept of two-way evolution" (*GK*, p. 167), and curiously remarks about "hideous beasts, like Lina," that "those on the way up are better than those on the way down, a profoundly depressing way of saying that animals are really better than human beings" (*GK*, p. 177). Reis uses the term "spiritual education" to discuss MacDonald's concept of "man's life as a stepwise progress of cumulative enlightenment" (p. 125). The essential consideration is the strength of MacDonald's emphasis on the spiritual aspect of man. MacDonald is saying people grow or diminish in the very spiritual quality of their beings, and that a certain quality of being is prerequisite to the understanding of any spiritual truth. The more one grows into spiritual maturity, the more truths he is able to receive.

Glowing, Flaming Roses, Red and White

as it does because of the mysterious antagonism of the human will to His loving purpose. The tendency of men is to "go down hill to the animals' country," as the old queen above says. In His working with men, God does not force Himself upon them, violating their wills; in so doing He would render men something less than human. On the contrary, God, who is Unfathomable Love, and who already has loved men into being by creating them, envelopes them with His influences, purposing their growth into higher conditions of life. But in this particular earthly life only some respond. And their growth into greater life is not easy; it may be painful, because it requires their being purged from all that is antagonistic to God within them.

Men's restless dissatisfaction with their present existences together with their pervading ignorance concerning spiritual truth arise from their need for greater life. God is the source and fountainhead of all life, and all of history is the story of God's "divine agony to give divine life" to His creatures. When men imagine themselves weary of life, it is in truth death — or apartness from God — that they are weary of. God's great task is to arouse men to choose the life that is in Him, and His working in creation and in history is all to this end. Christ came that men "may have life, and have it abundantly" (John 10:10).

As the two fantasies that are before us will illustrate, an individual is imperfect and spiritually ignorant according to how far he stands from the fullness of life into which he can grow. In the symbolism of the fantasy, life retrogressing from God may be reborn in another life as animal. But all that happens to the rebellious soul is calculated to effect its eventual repentance and turning toward God. Evil will continue to plague man and to hideously distort his spirit until the turning occurs. One day the retrogressing soul may come to see himself as he truly is in God's sight, and, having come to the end of himself, will turn toward God. The experience of *Lilith*, portrayed in MacDonald's final fantasy for adults, affords us the prime illustration of this rebirth.

MacDonald often uses Christ's parable of the prodigal son to illustrate this concept. It is to him the central parable of Christianity, offering the basic pattern of spiritual experience for all men. Eternal Love will not be defeated, nor its energies finally wasted. Curdie's Lina, the grotesque but devoted animal that serves him so well in *The Princess and Curdie*, is one of MacDonald's prodigals: he is a soul that, having retrogressed, has now turned and begun the long spiritual trek of becoming godlike.

GOD'S HOLY LOVE

Although love is the most basic of God's attributes, it is not expressed at the expense of God's holiness. MacDonald consistently takes the sternest view of sin and insists that God in nowise overlooks evil in men nor minimizes its consequences. All that displeases God in His children must be purged — not simply punished, for punishment's sake — and God's love effects the purging. In a sermon based upon Hebrews 12:29, "Our God is a consuming fire," he explains:

> Nothing is inexorable but love. Love which will yield to prayer is imperfect and poor. Nor is it then the love that yields, but its alloy. . . . For love loves unto purity. Love has ever in view the absolute loveliness of that which it beholds. Where loveliness is incomplete, and love cannot love its fill of loving, it spends itself to make more lovely, that it may love more; it strives for perfection, even that itself may be perfected —not in itself, but in the object. . . .
>
> Therefore, all that is not beautiful in the beloved, all that comes between and is not of love's kind, must be destroyed.
>
> And our God is a consuming fire.

This fire, then, is the very nature of God as it affects man. It is remedial in nature, ever seeking to refine man, so that he will become more godlike. God's true children desire the work of this burning within them, relieving them of what is antagonistic to God in their inner beings. They therefore go toward God, cooperating with the process as best they know how. The rebellious will experience this fire in the next world more directly than they do in this one. The consuming fire of God eventually will consume all evil. But, as the chief spiritual mentor in *Lilith* explains, "Annihilation itself is no death to evil. Only good where evil was is evil dead. An evil thing must live with its evil until it chooses to be good. That alone is the slaying of evil." Evil men must come to choose good freely, not by coercion, and all evil within them must be replaced, by the process of growth, with good.

God's wrath, then, is hardly distinguishable from His love: both are creative. The anger of God is not on the side of a holiness that is sterile and Pharisaical, and that feels somehow it has an exclusive claim upon God's love and mercy — the holiness, as MacDonald saw it, of many Scottish Calvinists. God is against evil wherever it exists, evil which encrusts itself upon seemingly righteous people in subtle ways. But it is consumable, and must be consumed, that the essential nature of man, the image of God, may appear. When man is fully purged, then he will be a son of God in truth.

These ideas are thoroughly presented in MacDonald's sermons, and they are embodied throughout his imaginative writings. *Lilith* offers us the most elaborate as well as the most explicit presentation of them. The symbolism in the two fantasies for children, *The Princess and the Goblin* and *The Princess and Curdie*, does not detail the entire process of spiritual growth, but it shadows forth many of these ideas. The great-great-grandmother, Queen Irene, and the manner of her working in the lives of spiritually sensitive individuals, the many types of creatures that arrange themselves on a scale of becoming, the strange fire of roses and its gift of "sensitive hands" bestowed upon Curdie — all these are pertinent to MacDonald's doctrine of becoming. In the manner of true art, these symbols do more than describe or illustrate these ideas: they present themselves imaginatively in a way that makes us *feel* their plausibility and power.

THE PRINCESS AND THE GOBLIN (1872)

Students of MacDonald tend to be fascinated with the extent to which his symbolic handling of the human psyche seems to

33

anticipate Freud.[2] The hierarchy of the ancient grandmother, the princess, and the goblins does seem to suggest the superego, ego, and id, and the house in which all have a part, the human mind. But one should be careful to integrate this insight with MacDonald's spiritual and moral concerns.

The theme of this fantasy is that one must have a certain inner quality — a keen sensibility and childlike naiveté — in order to discern the spiritual nature of the universe and to maintain a trusting, joy-giving contact with higher spiritual powers that work for the good of man. We will see in a later chapter how Anodos, the hero of *Phantastes*, upon entering Faerie, could see the fairies in the wood only because he had the fairy nature. So in this story, an inner sensitivity is requisite to spiritual health and growth.

The story presents a range of being, and hence of sensitivity, according to spiritual states, from the goblins — our baser selves — on the one hand to the old queen grandmother — our highest — on the other. The goblins are boorish, coarse-minded, and bungling, defeated by their own schemes, whereas the grandmother is altogether lovely and attractive. One of the most noteworthy aspects of MacDonald's talent is his ability to make good characters attractive, and this old lady is a good example.[3] Between these two extremes the other characters lie, and we like them to the degree that they are most like the grandmother queen, and least like the goblins.

In the symbolism of the fantasy, Queen Irene is a surrogate for the highest expression of being within man: God. She is Irene's grandmother — many times removed — and also named

---

[2]Reis, for instance, writes, "The Freudian hierarchy of ego (the Princess), superego (the Fairy Grandmother in the attic), and id (the Goblins in the basement) is obvious enough; and their presence reflects MacDonald's independent discovery of these phenomena" (p. 81). See pp. 41-45 for his discussion of the way in which MacDonald is one of those poets who "discovered" the subconscious prior to Freud.

[3]Speaking of the novels, Lewis writes: "One rare, and all but unique, merit . . . must be allowed. The 'good' characters are always the best and most convincing. His saints live . . ." (*Anthology*, p. 18).

Glowing, Flaming Roses, Red and White

Irene, because the highest human, the quintessential Irene, is divine, being made in God's image. Perhaps the definitive presentation of this view of the nature of man occurs in *Lilith*. The grandmother lives a mysterious life apart in the highest recesses of the house, but the mystery of her activities becomes a source of utter delight to those who come to know about them. Her pervading reality subsumes all aspects of the lives of those who love and obey her, as she constantly works for their good, their spiritual betterment. The realization of this good, however, depends upon faith and obedience. Many have not the inner spiritual eyes that can see her, and sometimes even those who do have eyes seek and do not find her, a momentary failure that may be due to some disobedience or neglect of one's present duty. MacDonald's emphasis is ever upon the necessity for active obedience that springs from childlike trust, and this children's fantasy, together with its sequel, gives particularly compelling expression to this necessity.

One must note, however, that these meetings with the old queen come at her bidding, not the princess's, and they are not simply the product of the princess's fancy. Rather, they occur to a person in "real life" when they are necessary to give him strength and instruction for a certain task. The king, though of sufficient sensibility, is not required, as the princess is, to have an active role in the task depicted in this tale, and thus, although he is on good terms with the queen, she does not appear to him here like she does to the princess. He explains to Irene: " 'She has not invited me, you know, and great old ladies like her do not choose to be visited without leave asked and given.' "

People like Lootie, on the other hand, live by a skepticism that precludes their receiving such visits; she remains in spiritual dullness. She is, therefore, a threat to the princess's relation to the queen and hence must be told nothing about the experiences the princess is having with her. The danger she poses is that of dismissing the reality of the encounters, calling them mere dreams, and influencing the princess not to take them seriously. MacDonald persistently sees this skeptical rationalism that precipitates doubt as the greatest threat to healthy spirituality. The shadow image in *Phantastes* is the clearest case in point.

The opposite of this skepticism is the simply childlike spirit. When the princess asks her grandmother about the moon that is always shining upon her, she tells the wondering girl that " 'if the light were to go out, you would fancy yourself lying in a bare garret, on a heap of old straw, and would not see one of the pleasant things around about you all the time.' " The moon seems to suggest the light of the pure, childlike imagination, without which the princess could not see the queen. The imagination is not unlike faith in MacDonald's thought; they seem to work together to achieve spiritual insight.

But even people who are on their way to becoming mature in goodness cannot see the old queen until they arrive at a certain state of sensitivity and openness to the supernatural. The experience of Curdie illustrates the point well. Perhaps the most fascinating scene in *The Princess and the Goblin* is that in which the princess with great expectation and enthusiasm takes Curdie to see the queen grandmother, only to discover to her chagrin that Curdie can see only a bare garret, a heap of musty straw, a sunbeam, and a withered apple. But Curdie is a boy made of the right stuff, and his encounter with the queen in the close of the story is promising. It furnishes a handy base upon which MacDonald can build a sequel, which he does some ten years afterward in *The Princess and Curdie*.

THE PRINCESS AND CURDIE (1883)

The sequel opens by recalling the situation that pertained in the prior story. A year has passed, the king and his princess have moved away to the capital, Gwyntystorm, and Curdie is sinking into spiritual commonplaceness. He believes less and less in the "things he had never seen," thinking they belong to dreams and not to the real world. Returning one evening from the mines with his bow and arrow, he shoots a beautiful snow-white pigeon. Immediately he is conscience-striken. Then, a bright light shines

Glowing, Flaming Roses, Red and White

around him from a silvery moon, beckoning him to climb the tower in the castle and come into the presence of Queen Irene. He obeys, the wounded pigeon in his hand. She helps him to see himself as having lapsed into a state of being on the side of wrong simply because he was "never wanting or trying to be better," but always pleasing himself. She then points him, in a series of interviews, to the path of true spiritual development.

Chapters Three through Eight, in which Curdie's interviews are presented, give graphic imaginative expression to MacDonald's view of the nature of repentance, conversion, and faith. Curdie comes to see himself as taking the wrong direction in life, turns toward goodness by a free act of his will, and places himself at the old queen's disposal, ready to obey her commands. She tests his intentions by making a simple request: he must never take sides with those who ridicule her. And when in any trouble, he must come to her. " 'I will see what I can do for you,' " she promises, " 'only the *canning* depends on yourself.' " MacDonald is underscoring an essential point: what divine power can accomplish for an individual depends very much upon the attitude with which he receives it.

Curdie's mettle is soon tested. The miners with whom he works begin telling tales of "Old Mother Wotherwop," attributing to her evil intentions and feats; they are clearly referring to Queen Irene, crassly misconceiving her. Curdie remains quiet, and is soon prodded and jeered for not agreeing. That evening, he lingers behind in the mine with his father when the rest of the miners retire. In the distance of the dark mine shaft, they see a pale green light, and, going toward it, they find themselves standing before the queen herself, appearing in the midst of an effulgent glory. To Curdie, "all he knew of the whole creation, seemed gathered in one centre of harmony and loveliness in the person of the ancient lady who stood before him in the very summer of beauty and strength." They are afforded this awesome and joyous vision because of the father's past faithfulness to truth and goodness, and because the queen has work for Curdie to do.

The Harmony Within • George MacDonald

When Curdie remarks about the difference between her former appearance to him as an aged grandmother and her present beauty and strength, she tells Curdie that different people see her differently, according to their moral state: " '. . . it is one thing what you or your father may think about me, and quite another what a foolish or bad man may see in me.' " She continues to explain that if a thief were to see her as she is talking to Curdie, he would think he saw a demon: " 'I should be all the same, but his evil eyes would see me as I was not.' " MacDonald seems to be imaginatively projecting a biblical principle, found, for instance, in Psalm Eighteen, in which the Psalmist says of God: "With the loyal thou dost show thyself loyal . . . and with the crooked thou dost show thyself perverse." That Curdie and his father see her as glorious reflects their spiritual state; that the miners had referred to her as Old Mother Wotherwop, a witch, reflects theirs.

Nevertheless, the queen tells Curdie that the next time he sees her he may not at first recognize the shape in which she will appear. He pleads for a sign by which he may know her, and she refuses his request: " '. . . That would be to keep you from knowing me,' " she explains. " 'It would be but to know the sign of me — not to know me myself. . . . No; you must do what you can to know me, and if you do, you will.' " Thus MacDonald suggests the tenuous and fleeting nature of the faithful soul's true encounters with deity, together with the way any such meeting is related existentially to one's obedience and childlike purity of expectation. The fixed rigidity of a given sign or image must not be substituted for real meetings with the living Presence. The interview ends with the queen's bidding Curdie to come to her in her tower the following evening.

Attempts to go to the queen, however, are often foiled by barriers and difficulties. It was so for the princess in *The Princess and the Goblin*, and it is so for Curdie. As he makes his way to the tower the following night, he is detained outwardly by a stern doorkeeper, and inwardly by a momentary distrust. The

Glowing, Flaming Roses, Red and White

figure of the self-appointed doorkeeper who would obstruct arbitrarily the path of the earnest soul is not an infrequent one in MacDonald's stories; apparently he means to condemn all clerics and ecclesiastical personnel who by various exclusive practices would interfere with, rather than help, those who seek God. This theme is more fully developed in the incident of the wooden men in Chapter Twenty-three of *Phantastes*.

Curdie's momentary distrust offers a larger threat to his coming into the presence of the queen. As he knocks on her door and is bid to enter, he opens the door to see only open sky and darkness, but no floor or walls. He stands dismayed, but decides to obey the queen's summons anyway, and as he steps forward, "that which had need of the floor found it, and his foot was satisfied." The scene may be viewed as vividly portraying the nature of faith, which is, as Curdie's example shows, simple active obedience to an explicit command, although the means to sustain that obedience may seem nowhere present to the human eye.

Within her presence, Curdie sees an Ezekiel-like vision of the old queen spinning at a great spinning wheel, singing as she spins, and the ultimate source of the song is Curdie's own heart. The song offers a dim prevision of a future joy and loveliness greater than human language can express. It anticipates the Resurrection — "the time when the sleepers shall rise" — and celebrates a universal restoration of all things. As the song ends, the queen laughs, and her laugh is "sweeter than joy itself, for the heart of the laugh was love." That this song originates in Curdie's own heart reminds us that MacDonald's view of human nature was somewhat different from that of his Calvinist contemporaries, who believed in total depravity.

Two images in the room attract Curdie's immediate attention: the Silver Moon hanging above, and the great fire of burning roses on the hearth. We have already remarked about the moon. The fire of "glowing, flaming roses, red and white" is the same fire by which the princess Irene was partially cleansed in the

39

prior story. That only her clothes were cleansed, and not her flesh, suggests that there is a spiritual readiness which she was not to receive at that time, her immediate task not requiring it. But Curdie must be prepared for a larger and more demanding task, and his preparation is painful and terrifying. He is now commanded to thrust his hands directly into the fire; the resulting pain is indeed as much as he can bear. Were he to have pulled away, we are told, he would have been killed; spiritual trials are startlingly crucial, and unless they are met with steadfastness, they take their toll.

When the pain eventually subsides, he withdraws his hands to find they have become white and smooth and tender. The queen tells him he has received a supernatural gift, whereby he is now able by a handclasp to recognize the true spiritual state of a man who is becoming a beast; such a person he is not to trust. Conversely, if he feels a person's hand as "child-like," he knows he may trust him, for, however physically repulsive the person may appear, Curdie will know that he is becoming better within. This gift will enable him to fulfill his mission.

MacDonald is building this scene upon principles very important in his theology. The fire of roses suggests that those destined by God to perform a particular task must first be spiritually prepared. They are the truly "elect," a term MacDonald understands to designate those who are selected to service, rather than designating in a Calvinist sense those selected for salvation from hell. This service requires preparation: "A man can do nothing he is not fit to do," MacDonald writes in *Lilith*. The preparation consists first of purging and then of the bestowal of any strength or special gift required for the execution of the task. God makes His servants fit for His work by purging them of what in their lives may displease Him. They must be holy because he is holy; there is no other way. But God enlists people to perform His tasks because in love He allows them to have active part in creating the good that fulfills His purposes, and He provides the wherewithal for any task He requires. The burning in the fire of roses suggests it all, and is one of Mac-Donald's more memorable symbolic scenes.

Thus the controlling idea in this scene stands at the center of MacDonald's doctrine of becoming. He sees no magic whereby men are changed suddenly and easily for the better, as too many views of Christian sanctification lightly suggest. To approach the burnings of divine holiness and be purged for true service is a costly experience to which only men of certain mettle are beckoned.

But one does not bear the pain alone. The experience over, Curdie sees the queen has been weeping, and discovers she had suffered with him while his hands were being readied for service. We are reminded of Isaiah 63:8: "In all their affliction he was afflicted. . . ." God suffered with his people when they were suffering. We will read in *Lilith* of the altar of "the Father's never-ending sacrifice for his children"; Christ's sufferings are as a coal from that altar.[4] The Christian can suffer because Christ suffered, because God the Father suffers, and will continue to suffer, until all evil is annihilated. "Much good will come" from it all, as the queen lovingly tells Curdie.

The whole process, however, is not without risk. Curdie could have withdrawn his hands from the fire, to his own undoing. And as he goes to fulfill his mission he is not immune from spiritual peril, for the queen warns him: " '. . . if any one gifted with this perception once uses it for his own ends, it is taken

---

[4]MacDonald's thought emphasizes that Calvary *reveals* the sufferings of God on behalf of men: "What Jesus did, was what the Father is always doing; the suffering he endured was that of the Father from the foundation of the world, reaching its climax in the person of his Son. God provides the sacrifice; the sacrifice is himself. He is always, and has ever been sacrificing himself to and for his creatures. It lies in the very essence of his creation of them. The worst heresy, next to that of dividing religion and righteousness, is to divide the Father from the Son—in thought or feeling or action or intent; to represent the Son as doing that which the Father does not himself do" ("Life," *US* II). He is very careful to repudiate any theology that posits a tension between a wrathful Father and a merciful Son whose sufferings pacify the former.

from him, and then, not knowing that it is gone, he is in a far worse condition than before, for he trusts to what he has not got.' " The threat of selfish motives negating true service is a constant one, as the queen again suggests in her final admonition to Curdie: " 'I have one idea of you and your work, and you have another. . . . You must be ready to let my idea, which sets you working, set your idea right.' " Clearly, constant deference to the divine will is requisite to success.

Thus prepared, Curdie leaves on his mission. His journey takes him to Gwyntystorm, the capital, and he finds the city to be in a state of spiritual degeneration, with the king and his daughter, the princess Irene, being held captive by usurpers. His task is to free the king and his daughter, and hence the kingdom, from destruction. How he does so makes good reading — this may be MacDonald's best long fantasy for children — but since the story does not contain much more symbolism, and what it does contain is an extension of what we discuss elsewhere, we need not linger over the plot.

Curdie completes his task in a city controlled by wicked men hostile to him and his purposes. When they are defeated, and the king is restored to his power, the king sentences them to be taken to the animals' country, with the pronouncement: " 'Now shall ye be ruled with a rod of iron, that ye may learn what freedom is, and love it and seek it.' " Not fit for this world, they are sent into a lower one until they learn some basic moral truths. Gwyntystorm, liberated from evil, enjoys a reign of righteousness under the new king and queen, Irene and Curdie.

The generation following Irene and Curdie's, however, reverts to greed and self-centeredness, and Gwyntystorm is completely destroyed: only a river and a "wilderness of wild deer" remain where the city once stood. MacDonald's visions, then, do not always end with the triumph of the good; the continual potential of the human will to turn away from God is existentially real. In this story, the evil enticement is a lust for gold, which shows the perceptive reader that man cannot serve both God and mammon.[5]

These two fantasies, then, offer provocative imaginative depictions of many of MacDonald's teachings on the nature of spiritual experience and growth. We need now to consider more closely his thinking about the way in which both nature and circumstance are continual means of grace working to accomplish God's intentions for man's spiritual maturation.

[5]Matthew 6:24. Woolf, convinced that MacDonald became disillusioned with his own understanding of life as he grew older, sees this ending as evidence that MacDonald is "in an apocalyptic mood, striking out at what he hates, and convinced that evil triumphs in the end" (GK, p. 176). But is not MacDonald simply reminding his young readers that the conflict between good and evil is continual, and thus if one does not keep growing spiritually, he retrogresses?

CHAPTER THREE

Outward Signs of
Inward Grace

" '*My boy! I doubt if you can tell what it is to know*
the presence of the living God in and about you.' "
—Mr. Graham in *The Marquis of Lossie*

The Princess and Curdie opens with an impressive passage of praise to mountains. They are "beautiful terrors," having emerged from the dark heart of the earth to stand majestic in the light of the sun. Inside, they are filled with rich deposits of ores and precious stones that silently wait to be discovered by man. As miners, Curdie and his father live and work to bring to light these "hidden things" and in so doing they are nourished and sustained. Their lives are reliant upon nature. This depiction typifies many of MacDonald's convictions about the nature of earth and man's relation to it.

We may use the term "sacramental," in a very broad sense, to describe MacDonald's view of God's relation to both the world of nature and the world of event and circumstance. MacDonald himself uses this term in a passage from his early novel *The Portent*, and in so doing gives us the kernel of his idea. He writes: "The very outside of a book had a charm to me. It was a kind of *sacrament* — an outward sign of an inward and spiritual grace; as, indeed, what on God's earth is not?" (italics mine).

A sacrament is an object or act that becomes a means whereby divine grace is, or may be, bestowed upon the recipient. Traditionally, Protestants reserve the term to refer to baptism and the Lord's Supper; Roman Catholics use it to describe seven essential rites of the Church. Whereas orthodox Christianity has tended to confine the application of the idea to very specific "sacred" acts, MacDonald suggests that it should have the widest possible application. Everything "on God's earth" is "an outward and visible sign of an inward and spiritual grace," in the sense that all circumstances and objects that surround a man on any given day of his life are invested by God with the potential to speak to him. Whether or not the potential that resides in a specific thing is realized by a specific man depends upon that man's present stage of spiritual development, his sensibility, and his attitudes. But God in grace is continually shaping outward circumstances to man's inner needs. "That which is within a man, not that which lies beyond his vision, is the main factor in what is about to befall him: the operation upon him is the event," MacDonald observes in *Lilith*.

In fact, all that is within a man sustains correspondences to all that is outside of him. MacDonald writes in *Orts*, a collection of his essays: "For the world is — allow us the homely figure — the human being turned inside out. All that moves in the mind is symbolized in Nature." These correspondences facilitate sacramental communication. A mystical life, a spirit from God Himself, courses through all nature and strives to communicate with man by using natural objects as symbols. In the novel *Thomas Wingfold* we read:

> All about us, in earth and air, wherever the eye or ear can reach, there is a power ever breathing itself forth in signs, now in wind-waft, a cloud, a sunset; a power that holds constant and sweetest relation with the dark and silent world within us. The same God who is in us, and upon whose tree we are the buds, if not yet the flowers, also is

all about us —inside the Spirit; outside, the Word. And the two are ever trying to meet in us. . . .

By virtue of the immanence of God in all things, as well as within man, there is a unity of substance between each man and the symbols he sees.[1]

MacDonald's theory of the nature of literary symbols is a direct extension of this thinking. As the poet uses images from nature truly, he reveals the thoughts of God resident in nature, and his work captures "truth in beauty" — MacDonald's definition for poetry.[2] The more a poet grows into spiritual maturity, the more his thoughts reflect God's truths, and hence the more potent his symbols become as sacraments. They are the vehicles of the truths God has given him to perceive and communicate. Further, in MacDonald's view neither the thoughts nor the im-

---

[1]*Thomas Wingfold*, Chapter 82. Reis sees antecedents for "MacDonald's views of God's self-expression in nature" in Emanuel Swedenborg, Jacob Boehme, and William Law (p. 38). Like so much nineteenth-century thought that speculates on the relation of the physical to the spiritual, MacDonald's conception derives in part from Swedenborg's thinking, such as is found in his *Heaven and Hell*. Greville writes that his father "knew enough of Swedenborg's teaching to feel the truth of *correspondences*, and would find innumerable instances of physical law tallying with metaphysical, of chemical affinities with spiritual affections . . ." (*GMDW*, p. 216; italics his). Thus Swedenborg seems to be the fountainhead of MacDonald's ideas, with some influence provided by Blake and Law. But his thought is most directly shaped by the German Romantics. Inasmuch as the French Symbolists also drew somewhat upon the thought of Swedenborg and the Germans, parallels may be drawn between the French Symbolists' idea of correspondences and MacDonald's. Yet in the material available to me, there is no evidence of MacDonald's drawing directly upon the French. The distinctive character of MacDonald's thought, and its chief interest for this study, is the Evangelical-pietistic emphasis MacDonald gives to this current of idea. Greville explains: "Once, forty years ago, I held conversation with my father on the laws of symbolism. He would allow that the algebraic symbol, which concerns only the three-dimensioned, has no *substantial* relation to the unknown quantity; nor the 'tree where it falleth' to the man unredeemed, the comparison being false. But the rose, when it gives some glimmer of the freedom for which a man hungers, does so because of its *substantial* unity with the man, each in degree being a signature of God's immanence" (*GMDW*, p. 482; italics his).

[2]*ADO*, p. 15.

ages conveying them may be said to be original with man. They arise from the "unconscious portion of his nature," and "God sits in that chamber" of man's being. Man in his subconscious being, therefore, does not exist independently from God. God made man out of Himself, MacDonald felt, and man lives and moves and has his being in God.[3] We will return to these thoughts in our final chapter.

One may remark that there is a large potential in MacDonald's thought for his claiming personal distinction and thus using his works to pontificate: "Stand thou there and be attentive while my works bless you." But he is never guilty of this. Next to the theme of the necessity for constant obedience to known duty, perhaps no theme is stronger in his works than that of the necessity of humility, the self-effacement that he himself tried to practice. He felt God allowed even the best of men but fleeting glimpses of truth in this life, and that men in future ages — who will be, he seems confident, more spiritually developed than in his time — will see truths still more clearly. The deepest things of God are "far too simple for us to understand as yet."[4] For these reasons he was content to let his works speak for themselves — but he does insist that spiritual health for any man depends upon his maintaining the closest possible bond between himself and his natural surroundings.

Many scenes in the novels and adult fantasies clearly depict these ideas about the sacramental relation of all things to man. Outstanding episodes showing man interacting with nature occur as Gibbie is in the thunderstorm in *Sir Gibbie*, and Robert Falconer is among the Alps in *Robert Falconer*. We can find other

[3]*ADO*, pp. 24, 25. "I repent me of the ignorance wherein I ever said that God made man out of nothing: there is no nothing out of which to make anything; God is all in all, and he made us out of himself. He who is parted from God has no original nothingness with which to take refuge. He is a live discord, an anti-truth. He is a death fighting against life . . ." (*Weighed and Wanting*, Chapter 35). Thus MacDonald repudiates the doctrine of creation *ex nihilo*, which Augustine taught, and which many orthodox theologians have believed. Cf. Acts 17:28.

[4]*ADO*, p. 18.

illustrations handily by anticipating some of the scenes in *Phantastes*. "All that man sees has to do with man" we are told in Chapter Twelve. Just after Anodos, the hero, leaves the Cottage of the Four Oaks, his first sojourn on his journey through Fairyland, and is walking through the woods, all the plants seem inhabited by fleeting presences that are interested in him. He observes:

> From the lilies, . . . from the campanulas, from the foxgloves, and every bell-shaped flower, curious little figures shot up their heads, peeped at me, and drew back. They seemed to inhabit them . . . and I heard them saying to each other, evidently intending me to hear, but the speaker always hiding behind his tuft, when I looked in his direction, "Look at him! Look at him! He has begun a story without a beginning, and it will never have any end. . . ."

All nature is interested in the being and destiny of Anodos.

In Chapter Twenty-four, after Anodos is slain in his noble attempt to battle the vicious powers of a religious ritualism, he is buried by his friends the knight and the marble lady "amid many trees," during the growth and verdure of springtime. In a monologue, Anodos tells us:

> Now that I lay in her bosom, the whole earth, and each of her many births, was as a body to me, at my will. I seemed to feel the great heart of the mother beating into mine, and feeding me with her own life, her own essential being and nature. . . . I rose into a single large primrose that grew by the edge of the grave, and from the window of its humble, trusting face, looked full in the countenance of the lady. I felt that I could manifest myself in the primrose; that it said a part of what I wanted to say; just as in the old time, I had used to betake myself to a song for the same end. The flower caught her eye. She stooped and plucked it, saying, "Oh, you beautiful creature!" . . .

He assumes other natural forms as well — in one instance becoming a cloud — and thus ministers to men. He exults that he now can "love without needing to be loved again," and he then expresses his newly achieved insights into the power and beauty of love, which we will consider in our chapter on *Phantastes*.

Anodos, being "dead," is able to realize experientially this power of love beyond any realization he had during his earthly life. The scene underscores for us the strength and extent of MacDonald's sacramentalism. Human attempts to love effectively may be hampered and rendered imperfect by the limitations inherent in the human condition; inanimate things may love with more abandon. In a scene near the beginning of Anodos's wanderings, in which he is enveloped by the arms of a beech tree, the tree croons: " 'I may love him, I may love him; for he is a man, and I am only a beech-tree.' " Removed from any suggestions of sensuality or self-advantage, the tree is able as a natural object to serve Anodos's present need to be loved more completely.

In the final chapter of *Phantastes*, Anodos is once again in his "bodily and earthly life," and the book closes with his seeking a momentary respite from his labor in the fields under an ancient beech tree. Reclining there and listening to the sound of the leaves in the breeze, he seems to hear them say: " 'A great good is coming — is coming — is coming to thee, Anodos.' " The fantasy then closes with this confidence: "Yet I know that good is coming to me — that good is always coming; though few have at all times the simplicity and the courage to believe it. What we call evil, is the only and best shape, which, for the person and his condition at the time, could be assumed by the best good." Even evil, in its effects, may be a word of God to a man. All MacDonald's writings may be said to have as their end the establishing within us of "the simplicity and courage to believe it."

AT THE BACK OF THE NORTH WIND (1871)

That evil, in the form of adverse circumstances and events, may be sacramental is a strong theme in the children's fantasy *At the Back of the North Wind*. The conclusion from *Phantastes* above would serve as an excellent statement of the controlling idea for this novel-length fantasy as well. The imagery of the title suggests the equivocal nature of adversity, the north wind being a common image for what is adverse and unpleasant. However, to be at its back — that is, going with it rather than against it — is, as the story soon makes clear, a fascinating and salutary place to be.

This ambiguous nature of adversity, with the possibility of its having a charming "other side," is graphically portrayed in the opening scene of the story. Diamond is the small son of a poor London coachman, and his bedroom is a rickety structure built over the coach-house, affording meager protection from the cutting blasts of the North Wind. One particular night when the rushing wind is whistling shrilly around Diamond's bed, he seems to hear it speaking to him. Engaging it in conversation, he discovers the wind to be a fascinating woman of mighty beauty, with both anger and sweetness mingled in her looks. From her face comes light, as from the moon. On succeeding nights he accompanies her, flying with her over London ensconced in her long hair, while she fulfills her assignments. She carries out the bidding of a Higher Power, whose ways she herself does not firmly understand.

When he is confident she is not cruel, but good-intentioned, he asks her how it is she can bear bringing disaster, such as her present task of sinking a ship. She answers that she hears above the noise of the immediate disaster the "sound of a far-off song" that quite satisfies her concerning the present suffering, for it tells her that "all is right." When Diamond objects that what comforts her doesn't do her victims much good, she counters: " 'It must. It must. It wouldn't be the song it seems to be if it did not swallow up all their fear and pain too, and set them singing it themselves with the rest.' " The principle that good can come of ill, thus illustrated in the opening scene, is then orchestrated throughout the course of Diamond's ensuing experiences.

Before the story reverts to realism, Diamond is taken to see the country at the back of the North Wind. The story makes clear that the trip occurs while he is seriously ill, and in a delirious state. She takes him far into the regions of the North, and then, in a memorable scene, he is commanded to pass directly through her person. Doing so, he enters a higher land in which nothing is wrong, but neither is anything quite right. This region, however, is pervaded with the certainty that everything is "going to be right some day." It is a land where there is peace and contentment intermingled with a patient waiting for a future fulfillment. The "good" dead are there, able to observe their loved ones back on earth, while anticipating fuller bliss in the Resurrection to come.

The experience of being in this higher land gives Diamond a moral and spiritual maturity beyond that normally acquired by anyone in this life, so that when he returns to health and the story progresses, he is shown to be a model of virtue. With impeccable obedience and industry Diamond works altruistically for the good of the poor, the sick, and the unfortunate — society's castoffs in the streets of nineteenth-century London. MacDonald's purpose is to show him realizing a fully harmonious cooperation with the principle already established — namely, that adversity and disaster are precipitated by a power that uses them as channels and instruments for an ultimate good to man. The concept itself is, of course, intriguing. But it is difficult, if not impossible, to work out in a believable manner in realistic fiction. For this reason, this section of the novel is considerably less appealing than the former section of fantasy.

It would seem, then, that symbolic art can succeed in suggesting the concept where realistic art cannot. For instance, the wanderings of Anodos in *Phantastes*, although they seem to be aimless and haphazard, and sometimes are terrifying, all work for his ultimate good, and the reader delights in the imaginative presentation of the principle in the fantasy world of Faerie. Similarly, as long as *At the Back of the North Wind* maintains a semi-fantastic setting, it also is charming and convincing; but at the point at which it seeks to demonstrate its theme in the real world of London coachmen, it fails to sustain one's acceptance.

This artistic dilemma is underscored by the success of the fairy tale "Little Daylight," which MacDonald nestles into the fabric of the realistic portion of the plot. A kindly poet who befriends Diamond visits a children's hospital and tells the patients there a fairy tale, the theme of which reinforces that of the book. " 'I never knew of any interference on the part of the wicked fairy that did not turn out a good thing in the end,' " the narrator announces, and proceeds to tell the story of a princess named Little Daylight. At her christening, a wicked fairy cursed her, dooming her to sleep all day and to wake only at night, and then to be strong or weak according to the waxing or waning of the moon. Thus she grows up into a beautiful princess, dancing in the moonlight forests but never seeing the sun. A noble prince, who sees her in her nocturnal dances, falls in love with her. Later discovering her on a moonless night weak and ugly because of the curse, he befriends her, completely unaware that she is the same beautiful princess he has seen dancing, and out of pity he kisses her. The spell is thus broken, and her beauty returns, together with the privilege of at last enjoying the sun and, it is intimated, the prince's love. This tale is pleasant and satisfying, temporarily suspending any reluctance we may feel to accept the larger thesis of the book.

The book itself, however, recovers its charm in the closing chapters. Diamond's illness returns, and he dies. North Wind resumes her nocturnal visits to Diamond during his illness, and his death is depicted as his making a final trip to the "back of the North Wind." The aura of her presence in these closing scenes lingers in the mind, and many of her speeches give memorable expression to some of MacDonald's basic ideas. For instance, she answers Diamond's inquiry about whether dreams are to be trusted: " 'The people who think lies, and do lies, are very likely to dream lies. But the people who love what is true will surely now and then dream true things. But then something depends on whether the dreams are home-grown, or whether

the seed of them is blown over somebody else's garden wall.
. . .' " Good people should trust their own deepest feelings and
treasure their own highest hopes. How they shall come to fruition
is a mystery, but one may safely hope they shall. Diamond ar-
ticulates this hope in a song about the seasons:

> Sure is the summer,
>   Sure is the sun;
> The night and the winter
>   Are shadows that run.

MacDonald's view of the sacramental character of nature and
event combines with his belief in the essential goodness of man's
primary feelings and passions to produce a view of human experience quite different from that of much of historic Christianity. It opposes the ascetic tradition and solidly challenges the
essentially Platonic assumptions upon which that tradition is
based. The view that there exists an irreconcilable enmity between body and spirit, and that the body must be severely
checked and chastised for the good of the soul, finds no sanction
in MacDonald's thought. For him, what men must pit their
spiritual energies against is the inferior selves of their beings, the
undersides of their natures. The enemy is within us, is indeed
our*selves*. These very important concepts are forcefully presented
in *Phantastes* and *Lilith*, to which we now turn.

CHAPTER FOUR

Wells and Cisterns:
Phantastes

> *"I knew now, that it is by loving, and not by being loved,*
> *that one can come nearest the soul of another. . . ."*
> — Anodos in *Phantastes*

C. S. Lewis tells of his first discovery of *Phantastes* and of the change it made in his life:

> It must be more than thirty years ago that I bought —almost un-willingly, for I had looked at the volume on the book-stall and rejected it on a dozen previous occasions —the Everyman edition of Phantastes. A few hours later I knew that I had crossed a great frontier. . . . What it actually did to me was to convert, even to baptise . . . my imagination. . . . The quality which had enchanted me in his imaginative works turned out to be the quality of the real universe, the divine, magical, terrifying and ecstatic reality in which we all live. [1]

Lewis had crossed into the land of Faerie, the land of all MacDonald's fantasies. It is a higher land, existing in the imagination, and entered by a willingness to leave our actual world behind and to follow the author on an adventure in which anything can happen.

[1] Anthology, pp. 20, 21.

54

Wells and Cisterns

In Lewis's case, apparently, MacDonald's theory about how this imagined land should function in the spiritual experience of his readers was valid. The authority for this theory, which we have discussed in the previous chapter in connection with MacDonald's view of the sacramental nature of all things — including the symbols of a truly Christian writer — lies ultimately with Novalis. The epigraph to *Phantastes* contains the essence of his view. (See the final chapter for a fuller discussion.) Briefly, this prescription for the construction of fairy tales calls for a narrative surface bustling and incoherent, supported by an underlying musical harmony. The subsurface harmony derives from an orchestration of themes, as I hope to show.

For a fantasy to function at its best sacramentally, MacDonald felt that a person should read it simply for his own pleasure, not consciously for his edification, as he would read, say, a parable. It is, of course, intuitive perceptions that MacDonald has in mind. Mere intellectual analysis alone tends to leave the spirit emaciated, not strengthened. He is confident that to the proper reader some incidents will seem to convey moral and spiritual truths; others will remain incorrigibly enigmatic. The type and quantity of truths perceived will depend upon the reader's spiritual state and special needs at the time.

Whether or not we approach the fantasy as MacDonald intended depends, of course, on the extent to which we are willing to accept his basic literary and theological assumptions. In any case, to trace the themes, as we are attempting to do, is to note the underlying harmony. In *Phantastes*, the main theme appears to address the problem of man's search for satisfactions for his personal desires and longings. The Christian concern arises because the natural process of seeking satisfactions for human desires is self-centered, and self-centeredness is spiritually destructive.

What is man to do? MacDonald does not advocate the classic answer of Christian asceticism — that human passions are to be repressed, and many natural satisfactions denied. He shows, rather, that it is better to serve others than ourselves, and that our desires can be satisfied indirectly through this service. Real love endeavors to give, not get, and in so doing, finds inner satisfactions that self-centered love cannot begin to know, together with a joy not otherwise attained. This theme is summarized in a poem found in Chapter Nineteen:

> Better to sit at the waters' birth,
>   Than a sea of waves to win;
> To live in the love that floweth forth,
>   Than the love that cometh in.
>
> Be thy heart a well of love, my child,
>   Flowing, and free, and sure;
> For a cistern of love, though undefiled,
>   Keeps not the spirit pure.

Spiritual maturity consists in being like a well that gives and is always fresh, rather than like a cistern that is full to stagnation. How one becomes the former and avoids being the latter is carefully illustrated in the hero's adventures.

THE HERO

The hero of the tale, Anodos, has various, rapidly occurring adventures in Fairy Land, each of which helps him to grow morally and spiritually. His name itself is instructive, being a transliteration from a Greek word which has two meanings: "having no way" and "rising."[2] Anodos wanders through Faerie in a seemingly aimless manner, but all that happens to him has the power to make him rise, or grow, so that he is in the process of becoming a better person. He enters Faerie when he turns twenty-one, and he remains in that land twenty-one days; in other words, having reached physical and legal maturity, he is

[2]Liddell and Scott, *A Greek-English Lexicon*, rev. ed. (Oxford: Oxford University Press, 1940), p. 145. An instance of ἄνοδος being used to mean the "ascent of the soul to its original source" is given from Hierocles Platonicus's *Carmen Aureum*. Woolf defines the meaning of Anodos's name as "pathless" (*GK*, p. 47), and Reis suggests "a way back" (p. 87). Manlove notes the meaning of "an upwards direction" (p. 275).

brought by his adventures to moral and spiritual maturity as well.

For growth to take place, Anodos must first accept the reality of the supernatural world. This requires both a certain inherent sensibility and a desire to cultivate it. At the beginning of the adventures, Anodos is concerned whether he has "fairy blood." and whether he can see the fairies in the woods. He learns from the lips of the country maiden whom he meets in Chapter Three that he could not have come so far in the woods if he did not have "fairy blood" within him. She takes him into the Cottage of the Four Oaks to her mother, who tells him that his ability to appreciate Fairy Land and to see the fairies there is determined by the strength of his fairy nature. He is much concerned about himself until he discovers that he can in fact see the fairies clearly. His fascination with their antics and affairs in the remainder of the chapter shows us that Anodos is indeed the right type of person to profit from these adventures. His having fairy blood does not, in itself, indicate that he has attained moral maturity; it simply assures us that he is such a person who may acquire it.

In Chapter One his attitudes and concerns reveal his need for spiritual growth. He is a young man who desires material and physical things. The story opens with his awakening in bed, and his morning thoughts concern his "legal rights," because he is in the process of inheriting wealth from his deceased father. He recalls that the day before, as he was searching through his father's things, he was interrupted by a visit from a tiny "woman-form," who excited within him certain desires, both admirable and unadmirable.

In his conversation with her, he makes three mistakes: he hesitates to believe in her because he has seen her only once; he belittles her because of her smallness; and, when she accommodates his prejudices and becomes "normal" size, he is physically attracted to her and tries to embrace her. These mistakes rest upon assumptions common to ordinary people in the world at large. The first is that the authority of any supernatural event is strengthened by the number of times it is repeated, an assumption to which the scientific mind is inclined. The second is that the larger something is, the more important it must be, an assumption made by dull minds in general. The third is that what is physically attractive must be immediately possessed, an assumption made by sensual people.

For these mistakes, he receives her rebukes. The rebuke to his sensuality is strengthened by her suggesting that she may be the spirit of one of his deceased grandmothers. The suggestion increases the mystery that surrounds her, and Anodos, looking into her eyes, is filled with an "unknown longing" for Fairy Land, which she assures him he will find tomorrow.

What is happening here must be carefully noted, for it suggests a pattern for much that follows. Two types of desire — the one for sexual gratification, and the other for joyous experiences in the supernatural world — follow rapidly one upon another, and both are associated with the same woman. MacDonald suggests that, for man in a low state of spiritual development, these two desires are not all that different from each other. Anodos must learn to distinguish carefully between them and handle each one correctly. This theme is worked out in detail in the episodes of Anodos's experiences with his marble lady, and is orchestrated in both the story of Cosmo in Chapter Thirteen and "The Ballad of Sir Aglovaile" in Chapter Nineteen.

One should note as well, in this important opening chapter, the use of male and female figures as symbols. The fairy woman tells Anodos: " 'I dare say you know something of your great-grandfathers a good deal further back . . .; but you know very little about your great-grandmothers on either side.' " Apparently, male ancestors symbolize the concerns of the everyday and commercial world; female ones symbolize the less known, mysterious side of experience. It is through the woman that one reaches to the highest truths — so elusive and difficult to express, yet so nourishing to the spirit of man — that give meaning to existence. One recalls the presentation of the female figure in the Curdie books and in *At the Back of the North Wind*: in the former, the aged queen Irene is both the essential human and the divine; in the latter, the North Wind acts as Diamond's entrance into the higher realm of life beyond death. Frequently in the fantasies, women have finer natures and keener sensibilities than men, guarding truth and guiding men to it. Therefore, physical desires which men feel toward women, kept chaste and tastefully expressed, are ready symbols of man's deep longing to possess a knowledge of ultimate truth.[3]

MacDonald, then, presents two attitudes toward sexual desire. In its baser form as lewd and promiscuous desire, he condemns it as being a certain evidence of need for moral and spiritual development. But in its higher expressions — regulated according to Christian principles — it is an aid to moral and spiritual development. Elsewhere in his writings (see, for instance, the essay "Individual Development" in *Orts*, or the novel *Paul Faber, Surgeon*), he makes clear that a proper sensuality may become a means of renewing one's conviction of the reality of the spiritual world. Many today may see this distinction of two types of sensuality as curious, but MacDonald sees a large difference between them and would argue that his interpretation is biblically sound.

FIRST ADVENTURES

We believe with delight in Anodos's entrance into Faerie, feeling wonder with him as the items in his bedroom gradually change into the natural surroundings of the new land. As soon as he is within this land of the imagination, he meets a country maiden who warns him concerning the trees: " 'Trust the Oak, and the Elm, and the great Beech. Take care of the Birch, for though she

[3]Joseph Sigman, "Death's Ecstasies: Transformations and Rebirth in George MacDonald's *Phantastes*," *English Studies in Canada*, 2 (Summer 1976), 203-36, offers an alternate interpretation. He explores similarities between *Phantastes* and Jungian psychology, and suggests that the male and female images symbolize the conscious and subconscious aspects of Anodos's psyche.

is honest, she is too young not to be changeable. But shun the Ash and the Alder; for the Ash is an ogre — you will know him by his thick fingers; and the Alder will smother you with her web of hair, if you let her near you at night.' " The warning is dramatic, preparing us for fierce conflicts between good and evil beings, both interested in Anodos's allegiances. In Anodos's later meeting with the beech tree, we learn of "an old prophecy" that trees will one day become men and women. Clearly the life that animates all of nature is full of significance for man, both for the present and the future.

Four oak trees form the corners of the first cottage he sees, indicating the trustworthiness of the country maiden's mother who dwells there. She, too, warns him about the ash tree, but avoids being specific about the danger; all she will say is that the ash's favorite tactic is to kill his victims with fright. The reader is deep within the story before he discovers the precise nature of the evil that the ash represents: the spiritual disaster which comes from being consumed with a selfish sensuality.

Another important person in Anodos's spiritual education is now introduced — the knight, Sir Percival. In the cottage Anodos discovers a large old book containing "many wondrous tales of Fairy Land," and in it he reads a fragment of the legend of Sir Percival. It pictures Sir Galahad, in wondrously shining armor, meeting Sir Percival, whose armor is red with rust and whose horse is "smirched with mud and mire." Percival's condition is a result of his seduction by the "damosel of the alder-tree." The account reinforces the warning given Anodos concerning the evil trees and suggests the danger he too will face.

Fleeing in horror from the spirit of the pursuing ash tree, Anodos stumbles and falls, stunned, at the root of a large beech. Suddenly he is enveloped by "two large soft arms" and hears the reassuring voice of a woman murmuring, "I may love him, I may love him; for he is a man, and I am only a beech tree' " (an incident described in the previous chapter). After giving him a tress of her hair to protect him from the dangers of the ash, she sings:

Wells and Cisterns

I saw thee ne'er before;
I see thee never more;
But love, and help, and pain, beautiful one,
Have made thee mine, till all my years are done.

Love that gives of itself—that helps another though that help means personal pain—unlocks the secret of life and bliss. This, Anodos comments, is the "secret of the woods, and the flowers, and the birds." It is a far cry from the love that desires to possess another for the satisfaction of selfish passions.

Spiritually exhilarated by this experience, Anodos next discovers his marble lady. While walking through a seemingly friendly portion of the wood, he enters a mossy cave for rest. He begins to daydream, thinking about "lovely forms, and colors, and sounds," until he realizes he is lying on a moss-covered block of alabaster. When he removes the moss from his couch, he is startled to find that it encases the marble form of a sleeping woman; she is perfectly lovely. Seized with a deep desire to awaken the woman, he finds himself "rejoicing in a song" and begins to sing. The power of his songs is effective; she arises and flees, with Anodos following. (We will consider in our final chapter why MacDonald refers so often in his writings to the power of song.)

The incident pictures Anodos possessed by desire or love in its highest and purest form. The marble lady appears to symbolize the spirit of the Ideal, or the Perfect, and, as such, is in MacDonald's thought a surrogate for the divine Presence. She is the spirit that weds perfect beauty and ultimate truth. Something deep within Anodos's soul answers to her: he comments that her perfect loveliness was "more near the face that had been born with me in my soul, than anything I had seen before in nature or art." These deep longings toward the Ideal which men feel have often been prime motivations for artists, and much of what MacDonald is saying in *Phantastes* intrigues those who are interested in a Romantic theory of art. At the time he wrote

61

Phantastes, MacDonald was the fledgling artist, with growing convictions about the power of literary art to perceive and express spiritual truths. Anodos mirrors him: he is a singer whose songs have on this occasion freed the marble lady, and will evoke her later. But readers who are not artists need not feel as though the symbolism applies to them only in a secondary sense. Anyone who entertains an ideal and expends his energies pursuing it will find that Anodos's experiences serve as a mirror, showing him much about himself.

FACING INITIAL DANGERS

The ideal is fleeting and elusive. One is compelled to follow by the love he feels for it, but the way is beset with spiritual pitfalls. Each pitfall Anodos faces is a variation on the theme of the nature of love. When love's energies flow exclusively toward the self, they are spiritually disastrous; only when its energies flow outward, so that all self-centered considerations are obliterated, can one commune satisfyingly with his ideal. The end of such selfless devotion to the ideal is union with it. Anodos summarizes at the end of Chapter Twenty-two what he learns: ". . . my ideal soon became my life; whereas, formerly, my life had consisted in a vain attempt to behold, if not my ideal in myself, at least myself in my ideal."

The first of Anodos's vain attempts to selfishly possess the ideal results in his falling into the hands of the Maid of the Alder. After he again meets Sir Percival, who warns him to beware of her, he resolves to profit from the knight's example, but nevertheless goes straight to his undoing. He composes another song, and a white lady immediately appears. The substance of the song, however, is quite different from the theme of the former ones: it addresses the "Queen of the Night" and asks to be secluded with her in a night of love. On the story level, Anodos is showing the same animal sensuality that he showed in the opening chapter toward his "grandmother" from Faerie. MacDonald has already warned against such passion, and will continue to do so in many episodes yet to come.

In this episode, the reader is subtly but definitely made concerned for Anodos's safety. First, in his song he dismisses the moon, hoping it will not rise this particular night. A frequent and complex symbol in MacDonald's writings, the moon here seems to suggest the beneficent providence of God that pervades the universe. For Anodos, it functions throughout his adventures as his guardian spirit. For him to dismiss it indicates he is laying himself open to danger. As he does so he feels a certain uneasiness, but he ignores it, yielding to the sensuous pull of the moment.

As Anodos's beautiful companion takes him to her grotto, he is enchanted with her "intense loveliness" and "extreme beauty." His sensual longings show him to be in a spiritual state of complete self-centeredness. Lying entranced with her loveliness, he is engrossed in the tale she tells him, in which he and she are the principal characters. He becomes ecstatic as he surrenders himself to self-centered imaginings.

But Anodos awakes from his swoon in the gray dawn to be confronted with horror. (In the dream world of Faerie, beauty and ugliness, the ethereal and the grotesque, can be swiftly juxtaposed without offending the reader's credulity.) His enchantress appears now at the mouth of the cave "like an open coffin set up on one end . . . a rough representation of the human frame, only hollow," tearing at hair held in her hands. She commits the terrified Anodos to her monstrously ghoulish companion, whom he now recognizes as the Ash tree. The ash, he now realizes, is the symbol of spiritual death, and his beauty is the famed Maid of the Alder, who has undone the knight and is now about to destroy him. About to be seized by the Ash, Anodos is narrowly saved when "the dull, heavy blow of an axe" echoes through the woods, and his would-be abductor shudders, groans, and then flees. His seductress, with a disdainful look, flees as well. Exhausted and dejected, Anodos, too, leaves the cave, a perplexed and humbled man. How, he asks himself, can "beauty and ugliness dwell so near"?

Thus the warning given Anodos upon entering Faerie is largely fulfilled: " '. . . the Alder will smother you with her web of hair, if you let her near you at night.' " So, too, the warning of the beech-tree maiden is fulfilled, who had admonished him there were beings in the wood resembling herself whom he should beware of, and he should try to avoid the "very beautiful." His unpracticed eye was deceived into mistaking the Maid of the Alder for his marble lady. He unwisely pursued what was beautiful for selfish rather than selfless ends. His mistake has almost meant his death, for all selfishness is spiritually destructive.

THE CHALLENGE OF RATIONALISM AND DOUBT

A related pitfall for one pursuing his ideal is that of succumbing to a sterile, analytical rationality. It may offer a challenge to the existence of the entire supernatural world, as the episode in the farmer's cottage does, or it may be destructively analytical of one's experiences, robbing him of the joy he should otherwise know, as the many incidents of the shadow plaguing Anodos suggest. In any case, this cynicism is a result of self-centeredness.

In the next adventure, Anodos accepts the hospitality of a farm family of four. The mother is a devotee of Faerie lore, and the daughter is fascinated with fairy stories; the husband, however, believes all fairy matter to be a hoax, and the son agrees, adding contempt to his father's denials. Through these two characters MacDonald shows the antagonism of empiricism and rationalism to all imaginative activities. The temptation is to disbelieve in Fairy Land altogether, viewing it as only a delusion. The farmer is the congenial "outsider" who simply lacks the capacity to perceive anything intuitively. It is ironic, of course, that he himself dwells in the very land the existence of which he would deny.

Leaving the farmer's family in a despondent mood, Anodos goes deeper into the forest and comes upon a hut, built against

Wells and Cisterns

a tall cypress (symbol of dejection), and enters. It is the house of the ogre, against whom the farmer has warned him. That the warning came from the male symbol of rationality suggests that no fine discrimination is required to avoid this danger. Anodos finds within a woman reading aloud from an ancient volume, a philosophy of negation and despair, the very opposite of all MacDonald himself teaches.

This dark philosophy, together with Anodos's mood, causes his cynical self to emerge. Probing in the cottage, Anodos comes upon a closet door which opens to "a narrow, dark passage." As he peers into the darkness, a "dark figure" runs toward him and, to Anodos's alarm, fastens itself to him as his shadow. The woman tells him that anyone who has come from a meeting such as his recent one in the forest is almost certain to be visited by his shadow. That is, Anodos there encountered his ideal — his marble lady — and he is now beset by its opposite, his lower self. Until Anodos masters the shadow with a spirit of humility at the end of Chapter Twenty-two (" 'I have lost myself — would it had been my shadow.' I looked round: the shadow was nowhere to be seen"), it intervenes and interferes in various incidents, defeating the good that could otherwise issue, and often working definite harm.

The theme of the possibility of many selves is a basic one in MacDonald's thought, and we will note its fuller development in *Lilith*. The "self" in this sense is not man's true person, but rather its negative underside, and control by the self is an open possibility for an individual, not a necessity. This idea is directly related to MacDonald's doctrine of becoming: each of the successive possibilities of inferior selfhood must be met and successfully denied as one journeys spiritually toward oneness with God. That Anodos's shadow emerges when it does is itself a mark of Anodos's spiritual growth, an indicator that he has so far advanced in inner development that his true self is beginning to be aware of a lower self that, when indulged, negates good and works harm. That the shadow most often expresses a cynical "common sense" or worldly-wise attitude underscores Mac-

Donald's insistence that a healthy Christian spirit is a childlike, imaginative one.[4]

As he continues his journey Anodos finds that now his relation to all things is affected by his shadow. When he rests on the grass, the flowers upon which he lies revive; those the shadow lies upon do not. His attendant appears "blacker in the full blaze of sunlight," and, as Anodos's fascination for his shadow increases, it becomes so bold as to smite "the great sun in the face." The sun seems to be a symbol for God, the source of all spiritual light; the shadow is doubt, rooted in rational analysis.

Succeeding incidents in Chapter Nine reveal the shadow's disastrous effects: he transforms the mysterious into the commonplace, and creates distrust between friends. Soon Anodos begins to think the shadow is indispensable to his well-being. He says to himself:

> In a land like this, with so many illusions everywhere, I need his aid to disenchant the things around me. He does away with all appearances, and shows me things in their true color and form. And I am not one to be fooled with the vanities of the common crowd. I will not see beauty where there is none. I will dare to behold things as they are. And if I live in a waste instead of a paradise, I will live knowing where I live.

This is the creed of the cynic, a result of a "common sense" approach to life. It is an avowed enemy of the visions of the imagination.

[4]After a presentation of the doppelgänger tradition upon which MacDonald seems to be drawing, Woolf laments that MacDonald shifts the symbolic significance of the shadow from "intellectual skepticism" to "consciousness of self" to personal "pride" (GK, p. 103). Reis agrees, concluding that the shadow's "symbolic meanings are multifold," but acknowledges a "subtle unity among the significances" (p. 93). He also sees similarities to Jung's "Shadow" archetype (pp. 116, 117). The point is, it seems to me, that these various manifestations of the shadow's nature are all consistent aspects of the cynical underside of Anodos's character with which he will contend throughout much of the tale, and which he outgrows spiritually through humility and altruism. Consult the sermons "Self-Denial" (US II) and "The Heirs of Heaven and Earth" (HG).

Wells and Cisterns

This conclusion leads Anodos to injure another by being crassly inconsiderate. In the forest he meets a little maiden, happy and dancing, who carries a small crystal globe. Touching the globe makes it pour forth a torrent of harmonious music. (It probably symbolizes the imagined story-world of a child's delight.) The girl is most gentle with the globe, but Anodos, emboldened by his shadow, seizes it, and it bursts. The child is heartbroken, and Anodos is thereafter haunted by the incident, until he meets her again later in his adventures.

Another result — but Anodos says he is not certain this one is owing to the shadow — is that people become grotesque to him when he gets very close to them: "I soon found that . . . to feel I was in pleasant company, it was absolutely necessary for me to discover and observe the right focal distance between myself and each one with whom I had to do." The suggestion is that human relationships are marred by a too-close analysis of what people are; to love one's fellowmen requires seeing them imaginatively, not only as they are but as they are capable of becoming.

THE FAIRY PALACE

Just as a stream flowing through Anodos's bedroom took him into Fairy Land, so now he discovers a streamlet which, as he follows it, leads him to the Marble Palace at the center of Faerie. Before he arrives, he is filled with joy, fed by his harmonious interaction with nature. The marble of the palace is like that of the lady he is pursuing, and we rightfully expect he is about to have experiences nearer the ideal than his former ones. These events further develop the themes we are tracing through the work.

Within the palace, he is pleasantly surprised to discover a room with this description on the door: "The Chamber of Sir Anodos." He enters to find a chamber the very copy of his own, with all his peculiarly individual needs met by "invisible hands." The incident neatly points up MacDonald's emphasis upon individuality in his writings. It stands in interesting relation to the emphasis upon community of the Christian Socialist movement — and the thought of F. D. Maurice — which, as we noted earlier, somewhat influenced MacDonald. God has made each man unique, MacDonald insists, and God intends that each maintain his uniqueness, that he might serve and worship the Lord in a way no one else can. The result is that each man both learns and teaches something of God in his relations with his neighbors.

On the third day after his arrival at the palace, he finds the library, and is delighted to discover that, in Fairy Land, to read a book is to become alive in the imagined world of history or fiction, or to become himself the philosopher in a book of metaphysics. In one volume he reads about a world in which children are produced not by sexual generation, but by a type of natural generation from the earth itself. As he explains the sexuality of earth to the inhabitants there, their reactions are mixed, but some long to die in order to be born into this world where they may know physical love. Though living in the Victorian Age, famous for its prudery, MacDonald does not hesitate to champion the role of sex, not as an end in itself, but as a means to a higher form of love, and hence, spiritual well-being.

But though sexual love, as distinguished from mere lust, may augment spirituality, it still falls short of what the imagination may envision as ideal love. This theme, together with that of the necessity to abandon all self-centeredness, is central to the tale of Cosmo, which Anodos reads next in the Fairy Library. MacDonald also uses the tale to probe further his concept of the nature of art. Thus he presents the story at this juncture to counterpoint the themes we have been exploring, and to indicate more firmly how each theme eventually will be resolved.

Cosmo, a university student in old Prague, has a mirror upon his wall which periodically shows him the image of a lovely woman. Falling in love with her, he uses magic conjuration to compel her to enter his own world. She rebukes him for his use of magic, and tells him she cannot be sure of his love for her or of hers for him until they both are free from all enchantments.

Wells and Cisterns

He must break the mirror, setting her free, though he thereby risks losing her. This he does, after a difficult inner struggle, but, in the convention of Victorian melodrama, he is wounded in the end of the tale, and dies in his princess's arms.

At the point in the story when Cosmo's fascination for the princess turns to passion, MacDonald quotes, without comment, this line: "Who lives, he dies; who dies, he is alive."[5] The climax of the tale neatly works out this paradox. Cosmo must be willing to destroy the mirror and risk never seeing the princess again in order truly to have her. He must completely relinquish his power over her before they can experience love on any other but a physical level; only this renunciation, a type of spiritual death, can open to him a higher experience of life and love. In this manner, the two types of sensuality are vividly illustrated in the story: the baser lust must be renounced, in order that higher love (which, like good dreams, is another means of grace in Fairy Land) may be experienced.

MacDonald's doctrine of the self comes vividly to mind, with the emphasis that he places upon the death of the self in his sermons on self-denial. In every phase of experience, denying indulgence in any pleasure that simply gratifies the self gives one a higher realization of the potential for true enjoyment inherent in that very pleasure. When Cosmo's love "withers" into passion, it becomes mere craving for self-satisfaction, and makes the princess a possession. To break the mirror is to give her her full selfhood; the love she will then freely choose to give him will be a much higher love. MacDonald will rework this theme very often in his fiction and make it one of the central themes of *Lilith*, as we shall see. To give one illustration from the novels, this theme occurs in the sequels *Sir Gibbie* and *Donal Grant*: in

[5]This line does not appear in the early editions; apparently MacDonald added it in a later revision (he frequently reworked his material). It appears in the 1905 edition (along with several new and fascinating illustrations by Arthur Hughes), published in London by Arthur Fifield. It also appears in the currect paperback edition (Grand Rapids, Mich.: Wm. B. Eerdmans, 1964).

the first novel the shepherd-poet Donal relinquishes the girl whom he loves to Gibbie, only to enjoy a yet higher experience of love in the second novel.

The second theme of the Cosmo story concerns the imperfect nature of any experience of love between the sexes. The tale is prefaced by a direct announcement of this idea: "Sometimes it seemed only to represent a simple story of ordinary life, perhaps almost of universal life; wherein two souls, loving each other and longing to come nearer, do, after all, but behold each other as in a glass darkly." (MacDonald is echoing Paul in I Corinthians 13:12: "For now we see through a glass darkly; but then face to face. . . .") Taken in conjunction with the previous myth in Chapter Twelve, this one implies that, whereas the love relation in this life is more complete than that of the existentially prior world of the myth, it is still imperfect and will perhaps in a succeeding world be still more complete. In the midst of relating Cosmo's tale, Anodos comments: "Nay, how many who love never come nearer than to behold each other as in a mirror; seem to know and yet never know the inward life; never enter the other soul; and part at last, with but the vaguest notion of the universe on the borders of which they have been hovering for years?" Cosmo's longings for his beloved can never be satisfactorily consummated so long as the mirror exists; nor can the princess be a free agent, sure of the truth of their love, until the mirror is destroyed. So, MacDonald seems to be saying, love relationships in this world fall short of perfection because of the limitations inherent in the human condition. That he sees this as universally true to human experience is probably the reason for the name Cosmo, from *cosmos*, meaning "world," and hence, universal.

The story of Cosmo also complements Anodos's quest for the marble lady. Cosmo's first fascination for the princess in the mirror is like Anodos's enthrallment with his ideal beauty in the marble block, and when his love degenerates into passion, it is like the sensual attraction Anodos felt for the Maid of the Alder. Anodos's continued pursuit of his marble lady, which is about

Wells and Cisterns

to be resumed, will also culminate in an act of renunciation, an act that is just prior to and necessary for his final spiritual maturation into full understanding of the basic moral truths of life.

DISOBEDIENCE, DESPAIR, AND DEATH

In the Hall of Statues in the Fairy Palace, Anodos again determines to evoke his marble lady through song. As he sings, she gradually materializes upon a pedestal, as if an invisible veil were being lifted upward from her. Overcome by her beauty and determined to "tear her from the grasp of a visible Death," he flings his arms about her. He is immediately rebuked, for he was strongly warned upon entering the hall not to touch anything. Fleeing from his presence, his marble lady disappears through a door he is forbidden to enter. He rushes through it, unheeding, to find himself in a wasteland, where, beside a great hole in the earth, he sits down to weep.

The Anodos who seeks to grasp his beautiful lady is not the Anodos in the grotto of the Maid of the Alder; his character has developed since then. In this instance he is prompted not by base sensuality, but by a determination to keep the lady in his sight.[6] His vision of her is of "the highest Human," which "faints away to the Divine," we are told in his song, and MacDonald in his published sermons develops the idea that humanity when it realizes its highest spiritual potential will differ in nowise from divinity.[7] Anodos wants to retain this revelation of glory he is receiving. But the momentary vision appears only in the context

[6]Woolf gleefully celebrates the eroticism he sees in this passage (GK, pp. 80-87). Here and elsewhere he seems to overlook the way in which Anodos's spiritual and moral development is shaping his behavior.

[7]"God is man, and infinitely more. Our Lord became flesh, but did not *become* man. He took on him the form of man: he was man already. And he was, is, and ever shall be divinely childlike" ("The Child in the Midst," US I; italics his). Cf. the ancient grandmother Irene in the Curdie stories, whose symbolic import is similar.

71

of his song; to try to compel it by an act of will is "in defiance of the law of the place," and he suddenly finds himself outside the palace.

Although despairing as he begins his trek through the wasteland, he makes a series of morally admirable decisions in response to his next experiences. He is now willing to relinquish his right to his marble lady in the presence of a "better man," and he sings a little song that summarizes an important lesson he has learned:

> In thy lady's gracious eyes
>   Look not thou too long;
> Else from them the glory flies,
>   And thou doest her wrong.

One must allow his visions their fleeting nature, and not attempt to capture any experience in order to prolong its effects.

Although he is no longer vulnerable to the appeal of base sensuality, as the next episode of the meeting with the elderly hag confirms, his self-centeredness is still present in his pride that it is *his* songs that have called the marble lady to life. This pride is stifling to his spirit. Crawling through a rocky tunnel, Anodos comes upon a gray and barren sea, the epitome of desolation. Overcome with despair, he determines to die. He walks out upon a low promontory, plunges headlong into the sea, and discovers instantaneously he has plunged into unspeakable joy. Death to the self is the final answer to pride.

References to water have been too closely associated with Anodos's crucial experiences for the reader not to suppose that water has symbolic significance. A stream of water flows from Anodos's bedroom into Fairy Land in the beginning of the tale, another takes him into the Fairy Palace, and a pool in a hall of the palace affords him a spiritually rejuvenating swim. Now in a sea he symbolically dies and is reborn. Similarly, water figures prominently in *Lilith*, as well as elsewhere in MacDonald's writings. Each association with water in Anodos's adventures marks his emergence onto a higher plane of spiritual existence, a transformation that generally occurs wherever one meets this imagery in MacDonald's works.[8]

THE BALLAD OF SIR AGLOVAILE

Anodos goes on his way, exhibiting an informed simplicity and confident childlikeness that MacDonald often associates with maturing spirituality. On an island after his sea journey, he enters a little cottage and is there ministered to by a woman whom he sees as both very old and very beautiful. But the beauty that Anodos now responds to is spiritual rather than physical, residing in her eyes and voice, so that he feels a "wondrous sense of refuge and repose." Having fed him, she sings him a ballad which repeats and develops the theme found in the Cosmo story and in Anodos's adventures to this point: that, since love and desire in this life are all but inextricably allied, spiritual death into newness of life is essential to be able to experience a higher love apart from base desire.

"The Ballad of Sir Aglovaile" begins with the knight Aglovaile's discovery, as he rides through the churchyard cemetery at night, of a ghost wailing a lament in the moonlight. Her song is certainly among the most charming that MacDonald ever composed:

Alas, how easily things go wrong!
A sigh too much, or a kiss too long,
And there follows a mist and a weeping rain,
And life is never the same again.

[8]In harmony with his Freudian concerns, Woolf sees Anodos achieving a return to the womb in his immersion, with water signifying "the maternal element *par excellence*" (*GK*, pp. 69, 70). In a footnote he dismisses Jerome Hamilton Buckley's discussion of water images in *The Victorian Temper* (Cambridge: Harvard University Press, 1951), pp. 97-105, as irrelevant to his interests (*GK*, p. 394, n. 17). But Buckley's discussion about the Victorians' inventive use of water symbols to suggest the spiritual new-birth is *apropos*. MacDonald's imagination is biblically oriented, and Scripture, not Freud, is the safer guide to his meaning. See especially the use of the water-life metaphor in such apocalyptic passages as Ezekiel 47 and Revelation 22.

The Harmony Within • George MacDonald

Alas, how hardly things go right!
'Tis hard to watch in a summer night,
For the sigh will come, and the kiss will stay,
And the summer night is a winter day.

This is the plight of the natural human condition. As the ballad illustrates, it is all but impossible to keep to the narrow path of truth and right apart from spiritual death.

Aglovaile discovers the ghost to be that of a woman whom he once had betrayed and who had died together with his child. When he exclaims about her transformation, she replies: " 'Thou seest that Death for a woman can/Do more than knighthood for a man.' " In response to his admiration for her beauty, she invites him to come closer, but with a condition similar to the one the marble lady gave Anodos: " 'Come, if thou darest, and sit by my side;/But do not touch me, or woe will betide.' " They enjoy for a time a blissful love, but the prohibition is one that Aglovaile cannot keep for long. Awakening from a dream in which she has fled him, he is overjoyed to find her still by his side:

And lo! beside him the ghost-girl shone;

Shone like the light on a harbour's breast,
Over the sea of his dream's unrest;

Shone like the wondrous, nameless boon,
That the heart seeks ever, night or noon:

Warnings forgotten, when needed most
He clasped to his bosom the radiant ghost.

As he takes her to himself, she turns into a corpse and disappears. Aglovaile is left only with the recurring lament which he hears "when winds are wild": "Alas, how easily things go wrong. . . ."

The simile above — the longing for the ghost girl suggesting the spiritual longings of the human heart — should not go unnoticed. The theme of the spiritual significance of love for woman is thus given another imaginative development. Feminine beauty answers to something deep within man that is quite other than

animal passion, but sensual man misreads his own spiritual longings, understanding them only in terms of physical desires. Physical love, when it is only an appropriation of the beloved for self-
centered pleasure, frustrates this higher purpose; yet man in his
lower stages of moral development cannot help himself. Spiritual
death and rebirth is the answer, for it results in a capacity to
love in an unselfish and outgoing manner. To MacDonald, the
passions are essentially pure and holy, but they "go wrong" more
readily than most other things. The further experiences of Anodos in the beautiful old woman's cottage continue to illustrate
this point.

THE FOUR DOORS

The woman's cottage has four doors leading outward, each of
which Anodos enters. Three of them lead him into environs that
recall past experiences; the fourth opens into timelessness. (Both
these adventures and others in the remainder of the fantasy seem
to refer to MacDonald's own past.[9] The woman tells Anodos he
may return to her whenever he sees her mark, a dark red cipher,
upon a door. At least two of these doors lead him to experiences
directly relevant to the themes we are tracing. Songs, which now
appear more frequently, begin to repeat the more basic themes
of *Phantastes* — namely, the nature of true love and the power of
death.

One of the doors is labeled the "door of Sighs." Going through
it, Anodos discovers he must assume second place to Sir Percival
in the heart of the marble lady. (The knight is morally superior
to Anodos, because he has been accomplishing good deeds while
Anodos has been, up to this point, passively learning.) Anodos's
noble response is to accept the situation, and to continue to love
her with an outgoing love. Returning with sighs of agony to the

---

[9]Both Woolf (*GK*, p. 104) and Reis (pp. 90-91) venture some specula-
tions about these autobiographical details. But, as Reis observes, to push
such reading is unwise, and does not add to the appreciation of the literary
merit of *Phantastes*.

woman of the cottage, he hears her celebrate further in song the beauty of this nobler type of love. The song concludes that it is better to express love like a well gives water, keeping itself pure and fresh by its endless giving, than to be like a cistern, growing stagnant and impure because it only receives for itself, without outlet. As we noted above, this nicely summarizes the major theme of the entire fantasy. The result of Anodos's resignation of his beloved to the knight is that he now loves her as he "had never loved her before." To serve is better than to appropriate to oneself.

After various adventures through other doors, Anodos is forced by rising waters to leave the ancient woman's cottage. Her parting advice to him is " 'Go my son, and do something worth doing.' " When Anodos previously overheard the knight and the marble lady talking about him, the knight had remarked: " 'There was something noble in him, but it was a nobleness of thought, and not of deed.' " Clearly essential to MacDonald's prescription for moral growth is action, the willingness to work out in life the duties one's conscience lays upon him by his recognition of truth.[10] Anodos's next adventures shows him nobly acting out the higher love, the nature of which he is beginning to understand. In a land exploited and tyrannized by three giants, he allies himself with the ruling family to break the power of the usurping monsters and successfully expel them.

Not all the effects of the "first worthy deed" of his life, however, are happy ones. No sooner does he contemplate his triumph than his shadow, which forsook him when he first entered the Fairy Palace, reappears, but in altered form. The feelings of pride his feat nourishes within him give rise to another severe spiritual peril.

[10]Reis speculates that MacDonald "surely adopted" his emphasis on active obedience from Carlyle's precept, *"Do the Duty which lies nearest thee, which thou knowest to be a Duty! Thy second Duty will already have become clearer"* (p. 41). But this seems improbable to me, given the difference between MacDonald's tone and Carlyle's bombastic tone, the pervasiveness of this type of insistence in MacDonald's writings, and the extent to which it is present generally in Scripture.

FINAL BATTLES WITH THE SELF

Absorbed in thoughts of self-congratulation, Anodos rides on through a forest "strangely enchanted." He is pleased to note that his shadow is not now with him, but he is startled to encounter a sinister-appearing knight who is the counterpart of himself, and who he suspects is one with the shadow. He is a "resplendent knight, of mighty size, whose armour seemed to shine of itself, without the sun." This knight is another of Anodos's alter-egos, possessed with a sense of self-sufficiency and independence from God, who threatens to enslave the true Anodos. The strength of his pride has given his shadow additional substance. In spite of all his prior adventures and the moral lessons each has taught, he succumbs to the trap; pride is the easiest sin to indulge. Finding himself helpless to do anything except follow his captor, he is imprisoned in a dark, dreary tower with a single small opening high in the top. When the moon shines in upon him, Anodos feels released; when the sun's rays penetrate the tower, he feels wretched and disconsolate. A dream of his childhood innocence and shamelessness increases his longings to be freed.

As previously suggested, these two planets appear to symbolize aspects of God. The sun suggests God's holiness — His love that is at once burning and life-giving; the moon suggests God's beneficent providence, an expression of His grace and mercy. One can readily see how God as the sun is displeased with Anodos's imprisonment in the cell of his pride, for it cuts him off from effective service. But it is not as easy to see why the moon should conflict with the sun, seemingly fostering an illusion. Perhaps MacDonald means to indicate that even though God in His holiness is displeased with Anodos's present predicament, He does not forsake him. God's mercy and beneficence are constantly extended to him in spite of his present folly, ready to turn this present trial to good when Anodos's humility returns.

Anodos is freed from his tower into the liberty of humility

through the power of song — not his own this time, but that of another. Opening the door and emerging into the open air, Anodos is startled to find the singer to be the girl whose globe he had broken, now become a woman able to sing powerfully. When he begs her forgiveness, she tells him she has nothing to forgive, because when the globe upon which she relied for song was broken, she was compelled to sing for herself — a valuable change. We recall the theme of the sacramental character of adversity developed in *At the Back of the North Wind*. This woman discovered her own talent through what seemed at the time a catastrophe. Her songs do people good, and her moral radiance is an inspiration to Anodos.

As she goes, she sings one of MacDonald's favorite songs, which appears here and elsewhere:

Thou goest thine, and I go mine —
  Many ways we wend;
Many days, and many ways,
  Ending in one end.

Many a wrong, and its curing song;
  Many a road, and many an inn;
Room to roam, but only one home
  For all the world to win.

To bring all men "home" is God's chief purpose and goal in His working in the world. In fulfilling it, He may overrule evil, creating good out of it. The main ally of God's working thusly, perhaps the very channel of His creating power, is love of the highest type, the outgoing love that through the woman has affected Anodos. Now he is about to go forth, doing deeds worth doing, motivated by his love. But first MacDonald takes the opportunity to reinforce the moral insights of the tale by presenting Anodos, at the end of Chapter Twenty-two, meditating upon what he has learned.

When he removes his armor, a symbol of pride in its subtler form, and leaves it behind, he discovers that now his shadow has completely disappeared. Its demise is simultaneous with his finally achieving selfless humility, about which he muses:

> I learned that it is better, a thousand-fold, for a proud man to fall and be humbled, than to hold up his head in his pride and fancied innocence. I learned that he that will be a hero, will barely be a man; that he that will be nothing but a doer of his work, is sure of his manhood. In nothing was my ideal lowered, or dimmed, or grown less precious; I only saw it too plainly, to set myself for a moment beside it. Indeed, my ideal soon became my life; whereas, formerly, my life had consisted in a vain attempt to behold, if not my ideal in myself, at least myself in my ideal.

Perhaps nowhere in his writings does MacDonald define more precisely the meaning of humility and the attitude of the humble man toward his ideal. Here is the fulfillment of MacDonald's epigraph to this chapter, taken from the writings of Cyril Tourneur, a dramatist contemporary with Shakespeare: "Joy's a subtil elf./I think man's happiest when he forgets himself." Not seeing oneself in his ideal, but rather forgetting the self through absorption in the ideal, marks the narrow distinction between pride and humility.

Even so, this humility does not effect the annihilation of all false selves. Another self arises in Anodos that takes pleasure in self-degradation; this false self, too, must die. MacDonald concludes: "Self will come to life even in the slaying of self; but there is ever something deeper and stronger than it, which will emerge at last from the unknown abysses of the soul. . . ." In *Lilith*, this idea will be compellingly symbolized in the scene of Lilith's "death," in which the spot on her side and the worm destroy all but the very essence of her being.

CONFLICTS WITH ANTAGONISTIC RELIGIOUS SYSTEMS

Anodos is now depicted as undertaking further deeds "worth doing." His spiritual development, which is progressing fairly

The Harmony Within • George MacDonald

well, is a means to an end, rather than an exclusive end in itself. MacDonald emphasizes in all his writings that righteousness is nothing unless it is practically expressed in good deeds; one must become a being capable of performing righteous acts by the process of *doing* them. The adventures of Chapter Twenty-three show Anodos acquitting himself admirably as Sir Percival's squire.

Two episodes particularly attract our attention. They illustrate the destructive effects that self-centered religious leaders and people in authority have upon sincerely seeking, childlike individuals. This knight tells Anodos that "notwithstanding the beauty of this country of Faerie . . . there is much that is wrong in it," and proceeds to relate the incident of the wooden men, which is followed by that of the forest chapel.

The first incident concerns a little girl who is in search of wings to enable her to fly back to the country from which she has come. She has but to acquire them from obliging butterflies and moths, but when she asks for them, she is trampled upon by grotesque monsters "like great men, made of wood, without knee or elbow-joints, and without any noses or mouths or eyes in their faces." The knight learns that to cut down these creatures with the sword only results in more pieces that join in the attack. He finally succeeds in thwarting them by tripping them and setting them upon their heads, which renders each helpless.

The wooden men seem to represent leaders of cultic mentality in Christianity. Their religious set of mind is inhuman (wooden), inflexible (without joints), and oblivious to the obvious (without noses and other sensory organs). Instead of helping the sincerely devout, who look to them to nurture the better aspects of their natures, these obtuse creatures do nothing but frustrate and hinder their spiritual aspirations. When attacked, they react by quickly producing others of similar mentality. The knight's solution — that of setting them on their heads, which renders them ineffectual — suggests showing them the intellectual shortcomings of their own system. MacDonald spent his life doing this, imaginatively in the symbolism of his fantasies and the realistic depictions of his fiction, and discursively in his sermons and essays.[11]

In the second episode, Anodos comes upon a portion of the forest in which separate trails of felled trees seem to lead to a "common center," and he and the knight enter a forest chapel with walls of yew trees. Within are rows of white-robed, priestly figures reciting liturgical chants, and a large, attentive crowd. The sun has set, and darkness prevails, pierced only by starlight. Young initiates are being taken by groups of the white-robed figures to the farther end of the long chapel, where a "majestic-looking figure" is seated high upon a throne; they are then coerced into entering a door in the pedestal of the throne, where they disappear.

The ceremony fills the knight with reverence and awe: "Incapable of evil himself, he could scarcely suspect it in another, much less in a multitude such as this." Anodos, however, his sight being "so much more keen than that of most people," suspects evil here, and, donning the robe of an initiate, makes his way to the front as though to present himself to the image on the throne. Arriving before the image, he boldly approaches and attacks it, hurling it from its seat. A "great brute, like a wolf" emerges from the chamber in the pedestal and attacks him, they struggle, and Anodos strangles the wolf. Anodos is, however, attacked by the indignant multitude of worshippers, and killed.

Institutionalized religion, with its strong centers of authority and more formal patterns of worship, may be symbolized here. In a manner remarkably anticipatory of twentieth-century trends, religious people appear to be exercising what MacDonald would identify as an injudicious tolerance — that of assuming all religions have a commonality in truth, inasmuch as all are expressions of the human search for the divine. Such "believers" fool the knight, but not Anodos, who actively tries to expose the emptiness of

[11]See the sermons "Jesus and His Fellow Townsmen" and "The Yoke of Jesus" (HG) for delineation of this religious set of mind.

their forms of humanism, and is killed in the attempt. To expose with purified motives and spirit the error of mistaken religious attitudes is, in MacDonald's thinking, close to the most noble deed the true Christian thinker can perform.

Such exposure is necessary, but not for the sake of creedal purity. It is important to notice in each of the above episodes that it is action based upon attitudes, not creedal errors, that is being condemned. MacDonald insists theology is not an end in itself; its end is Christian action. But wrong thinking — which invariably springs from wrong attitudes toward the self and which issues in mistaken conclusions about the nature and end of religious experience — produces conduct that is spiritually outrageous.

THEMES RESOLVED

In the closing chapters of *Phantastes* MacDonald gives final expression to the main themes that he has firmly controlled and developed throughout the story. The first theme concerns the nature of passion. Now "dead," Anodos is lamented and buried by his knight and lady. But, far from being unconscious, he is experiencing the bliss of a more complete life and love. (The theme of the nature of death, with MacDonald's view of its sanctifying powers, is also a strong element in *Lilith* and *At the Back of the North Wind*.) That which was coarse within him is now refined and pure: "If my passions were dead, the souls of the passions, those essential mysteries of the spirit which had embodied themselves in the passions, and had given to them all their glory and wonderment, yet lived, yet glowed, with a pure, undying fire. They rose above their vanishing earthly garments, and disclosed themselves angels of light. But oh, how beautiful beyond the old form!"

One is reminded of Sir Aglovaile, who mistook the soul of his passion for its physical fulfillment, and ravished the ghost-girl to his own undoing. The passions themselves are pure. In this life they can lead one astray swiftly, yet they are not thereby to be

despised; there is a "glory and wonderment" in them. In a future
life man will not be bereft of them, but rather he will be enabled
by his passions — then purified — to know the full blessedness of
"the land of Death." Thus MacDonald brings to culmination the
theme he has been exploring most persistently in this fantasy.

The next theme, that of the vital role of nature in spiritual
growth, also culminates in these closing chapters. *Phantastes* contains many key passages expressing this aspect of MacDonald's
thinking, some of which we have already discussed.

The theme of the nature and power of love, however, is the
focus of the penultimate chapter. Anodos discovers that he now
is able to love others without needing to be loved in return. And
he has developed a fuller knowledge of what love is:

> *I knew now, that it is by loving, and not by being loved, that one can
> come nearest the soul of another; yea, that, where two love, it is the
> loving of each other, and not the being beloved by each other, that
> originates and perfects and assures their blessedness. I knew that love
> gives to him that loveth, power over any soul beloved, even if that soul
> know him not, bringing him inwardly close to that spirit; a power that
> cannot be but for good; for in proportion as selfishness intrudes, the
> love ceases, and the power which springs therefrom dies. Yet all love
> will, one day, meet with its return. All true love will, one day, behold
> its own image in the eyes of the beloved, and be humbly glad.*

All love, including that between the sexes, is here defined. Base
sensuality — any form of appropriation of another for personal
satisfaction alone — destroys true love, because love is in its essence self-giving. The altruistic act of giving of oneself for the
pleasure or uplifting of the beloved brings blessedness to the
lover. It effects an intimacy otherwise impossible, a power to
do the other good, and, in the future, a still greater return of
personal likeness in the beloved.

BACK HOME

But Anodos's "death" is not permanent. With a "pang and a
terrible shudder" he finds himself transmitted back to the con-

fines of a "more limited, even a bodily and earthly life," and he returns to his castle to assume his duties as overlord of his lands. That he is now spiritually mature is indicated by the fact that his experiences in Faerie have taken twenty-one days, and that he has lost his shadow. His chief concern is whether he can "translate the experiences of my travels there, into common life." He muses: "I have a strange feeling sometimes, that I am a ghost, sent into the world to minister to my fellow-men, or, rather, to repair the wrongs I have already done." Because he has learned selflessness and humility, Anodos can now perform these deeds effectively.

CHAPTER FIVE

"I Wis We War A' Deid!": Lilith

"There is no joy belonging to human nature, as God made it, that shall not be enhanced a hundredfold to the man who gives up himself—though, in so doing, he may seem to be yielding the very essence of life."
— From the sermon "Self Denial," *US* II

Almost thirty-five years after writing *Phantastes,* MacDonald in 1890 began *Lilith,* a fantasy for adults that he intended to be the final imaginative embodiment of his deepest beliefs. Greville records that "he was possessed by a feeling—he would hardly let me call it a conviction, I think—that it was a mandate direct from God." When Louisa MacDonald read the manuscript and found the imagery obscure, her distress gave her husband "real heartache, so that he began to question his ability to utter his last urgent message" (*GMDW,* p. 548). MacDonald next consulted Greville. With his verdict that *Lilith* was the "Revelation of St. George [MacDonald]," MacDonald overcame his doubts, and the book appeared in final form in 1895.[1]

---

[1]Greville published *Lilith* as a centenary commemoration and included a paraphrase of the earlier manuscript version (London: George Allen & Unwin, 1924).

Lilith is more theologically oriented than *Phantastes,* and the weight of its thought encumbers it at times; apparently Mac-Donald was not as content as he was before to let the symbols speak for themselves. Nevertheless, it is an impressive performance. The central purpose of the work is to give symbolic expression to the idea that salvation is the process whereby children of God become sons through abandoning their old "selves" and being renewed in grace. Complementing this idea are MacDonald's convictions about the meaning of spiritual liberty, the destructive character of mere rationalism, the nature of evil, the function of sorrow, and the necessity of obedience. A certain quality of being is essential to spiritual freedom, to understanding, and to performing any truly good deeds. The moral of the fantasy is that all humanitarianism is vain that is not preceded by complete spiritual death to the self. It seems to me that *Lilith* offers the definitive interpretation of George MacDonald's oft-repeated desire expressed in his native Scotch, "I wis we war a' deid."

THE REGION OF SEVEN DIMENSIONS

MacDonald creates the reality of this other world and effects the transition into it with the same ease and skill that he commands in *Phantastes.* But the world of *Lilith* differs from that of *Phantastes* in that the reader has a firmer sense of "the interpenetrating yet unmingling" relationship that exists between it and our own world.[2] The hero, Mr. Vane, not only enters and returns a number of times throughout the fantasy, but Mr. Raven tells him that the two worlds are coincident and co-existent: " ' . . . you see that large tree to your left, about thirty yards away?' " he asks Vane. " 'That tree stands on the hearth of your kitchen, and grows nearly straight up its chimney.' " The hyacinths and roses

[2]Prickett, pp. 223-48, argues that MacDonald's concept of two interpenetrating worlds derives from Coleridge's doctrines of the nature of the imagination and of symbol. Also, it affords a certain anticipation of Charles William's doctrine of co-inherence, as found, for instance, in *Descent of the Dove* (Grand Rapids, Mich.: Wm. B. Eerdmans, 1972 [1939]).

growing in that world are responsible for the "peculiar sweet-ness" of the music coming from the piano being played in his home because they are growing coincidentally with the instrument.

The seven dimensions are formed by adding four spiritual dimensions to the familiar three. Greville credits Jacob Boehme, the seventeenth-century German mystic, with contributing to this idea, and notes that his father maintained some interest in Boehme throughout his life.[3] It is worth noting that these extra dimensions have not appeared in MacDonald's fantasies until now. Asserting the presence of spiritual dimensions appears to be his attempt to seize his reader's imagination with a sense of the overriding importance of life's spiritual aspects. After years of communicating his message to his Victorian world, he had apparently concluded that a still greater emphasis needed to fall on the reality of man's spiritual nature.

These coincidental worlds have only one common ground: morality. Mr. Raven on another occasion explains: " ' . . . most of its physical, and many of its mental laws are different from those of this world. As for moral laws, they must everywhere be fundamentally the same.' " The reader is required, then, to suspend his disbelief concerning curious psychic and material phenomena — asking only self-consistency in these areas — and to depend for his bearings upon his grasp of moral laws alone. When he does so he takes a firmer hold upon his knowledge of moral principles, and MacDonald neatly accomplishes his purpose of intensifying the reader's moral awareness.

MacDonald discourages further speculation about the locality of this world by suggesting that it may be entered by a state of mind — a book, for instance, is one door into it — and by treating the question itself with a certain contempt. Vane overhears two shades engaging in a dialogue which is rendered pathetic by virtue of their low position on the scale of becoming, and the

---

[3]*GMDW*, p. 557. In his Introduction to the 1924 edition of *Lilith*, Gre-ville explains these extra four spiritual dimensions as being "of Elemental, illimitable reach — like the four points of the compass, or the Four Elements in spiritual aspect" (p. xv).

one remonstrates: " '*Where* are we? Locality is the question! To be or not to be, is not the question.' " The reader is inclined to dissociate himself from the problem of locality simply because such a morally inferior being declares it to be important.

ARGUMENT

The hero's name, Vane, suggests both pride and futility.[4] At the beginning of the tale, he is spiritually immature, and in Faerie he wastes a good deal of energy on well-meant but futile activities. This futility is in keeping with MacDonald's theme that actions most helpful to others can only come from actors who have been spiritually prepared through death to their lower selves.

The argument of the entire fantasy is, in short, that spiritual death to one's inferior selves, symbolized by sleep, is essential to being and doing. When Vane first enters Faerie and meets Mr. Raven, his initial questions have to do with where he is. But the raven counters with what is the central question of the book: " 'Tell me, then, who you are — if you happen to know. . . . Are you sure you are not your own father? — or excuse me, your own fool?' " Vane is confused to realize that he has "no grounds on which to determine" who he is. He is soon told that he is but "beginning to become an individual" and that requisite to his continued becoming is his sleeping in Eve's charnel house. Later, after he has failed to help the Little Ones and is again talking with Mr. Raven, he learns that it is necessary that he sleep before he can do anything really helpful for them, because "a man can do nothing he is not fit to do."

Thus far "sleep" seems to suggest dying to one's lower selves. But it may also be seen to have another significance. Theologians have long disagreed about a perplexing question that this phenomenon raises: how the gap in being between that state of imperfection in which the soul dies and the state of perfect

---

[4]Reis suggests the meanings *vain* and *weathervane* (p. 95).

0

holiness required for full communion with God is filled. Catholic
theology teaches purgation in Purgatory, whereas Protestants
tend to argue for an immediate act of God in which the soul is
instantaneously transformed into the full image of Christ. Mac-
Donald seems to combine elements of both views. The individual
experiences in his final long sleep in Eve's house whatever further
changes are needed to travel "home to the Father."

Sleeping certainly suggests passivity, and perhaps MacDonald
means to stress that these acts of dying and the process of
glorification are such that the individual contributes nothing to
them except the willingness to succumb. The act of the will is,
then, all-important. To refuse to "sleep" is to retrogress on the
scale of becoming. One refuses if he is under the delusion that
becoming is a process of the soul making itself — that life consists
in doing as one pleases and becoming what one chooses. But he
who labors under this delusion makes himself a hideous entity
in God's sight.

The career of Lilith illustrates all this.[5] In Mara's house
on the eve of her surrendering to sleep, Lilith resists Mara's
patient efforts to bring her to surrender. " 'I will be myself and
not another,' " she insists. Mara counters: " 'Alas, you are another
now, not yourself! Will you not be your real self?' " Mara
continues:

"... but another has made you, and can compel you to see what you
have made yourself. You will not be able much longer to look to yourself
anything but what he sees you! You will not much longer have satis-

[5]Her name is a transliteration of the Hebrew term meaning "night-
monster." It appears only once in the Hebrew Scriptures, in Isaiah 34:14,
and this in a highly poetized passage. The Jewish mystics in the Middle
Ages, the Cabala, popularized her as a figure in Jewish mythology: Adam's
first wife. Reis remarks that they "apparently were trying to reconcile the
two different accounts of the creation of woman in Genesis" (p. 99), Genesis 1:27 and 2:21-22, and gives a helpful exposition of the myth. Roderick
F. McGillis in "George MacDonald and the Lilith Legend in the XIXth Century," *Mythlore*, 6(Winter 1979), 3-11, gives a thorough account of the
history of this legend.

*faction in the thought of yourself. At this moment you are aware of
the coming change!"*

*"No one ever made me. I defy that Power to unmake me from a free
woman! You are his slave, and I defy you! You may be able to torture
me —I do not know, but you shall not compel me to anything against
my will!"*

"Such compulsion would be without value. . . ."

The primary sin here is the pride of self-sufficiency and its
concomitant independence from God. The rebelling individual
persists in it until he comes to the end of himself, for the evil
that he has given himself to is by its very nature self-consuming.
Lilith now is being brought to an ability to make a free choice.
What she is being compelled to is the dismissal of all illusions;
only then can the will be said to be truly free. MacDonald is
convinced that the soul, freed from all false selves and all false
images of itself, will unerringly choose God. This is the ultimate
motivating consideration behind his hope for the salvation of
mankind. He is no fatalist. Men are not coerced into choosing
God; they will all one day simply be allowed a clear-sighted
choice.[6]

Lilith's great delusion is that in her self-sufficiency she is free,
and that to serve God is to be His slave, as she tells Mara above.
Mara answers her objections: " 'I am no slave, for I love that
light, and will with the deeper will which created mine. There
is no slave but the creature that wills against its creator. Who
is a slave but her who cries, "I am free," yet cannot cease to
exist?' " She further tells Lilith that her exercise of power, en-
slaving others to her will, has been in fact the very thing to
which she was herself enslaved. Mara's is a higher freedom, a

[6]See Psalm 22:25-31 and Isaiah 45:22-24 for two biblical passages that
may be seen as contributing to MacDonald's view. On the biblical basis for
the universalist hope, see William Barclay, *A Spiritual Autobiography*
(Grand Rapids, Mich.: Wm. B. Eerdmans, 1975), pp. 58-64. He discusses
such passages as John 12:32; Romans 11:32; I Corinthians 15:22, 28; I Timothy
2:4-6; and Matthew 25:46 as supportive of his own commitment to this
position.

freedom realized when an individual's will has grown through proper exercise to be in constant harmony with the God who created him. It is attained by the individual who loves the truth and is morally committed to it. Such a view of the nature of Christian liberty is essentially Augustinian.

THE WAY TO UNDERSTANDING

A certain quality of being is necessary for full understanding as well as for ultimate freedom (and neither Vane — nor Mac-Donald — has achieved this completely when the fantasy closes). MacDonald repeats in *Lilith* his contempt for mere rationalism that demands understanding prior to moral commitment, but at the same time he insists that the universe ultimately will be intelligible to the individual who is spiritually mature. When Vane first enters the region of seven dimensions, he sees a radiantly beautiful bird-butterfly, and pursues it:

> . . . *a great longing awoke in me to have it in my hand. To my unspeakable delight, it began to sink toward me. Slowly at first, then swiftly it sank, growing larger as it came nearer. I felt as if the treasure of the universe were giving itself to me — put out my hand, and had it. But the instant I took it, its light went out; all was dark as pitch; a dead book with boards outspread lay cold and heavy in my hand. I threw it in the air — only to hear it fall among the heather.*

This is the result of the craving to understand by rational analysis alone; to possess a mystery is to kill it. One is reminded of Cosmo in *Phantastes,* and the fate that befell him when he attempted to possess his princess. In both instances, a quality of being that is achieved only through spiritual death to the self, which involves a willingness to refrain from possessing a thing or a person for mere selfish pleasure, is necessary to understanding and enjoyment.

The universe, nevertheless, finally will be understood. When Vane chides Mr. Raven for talking only in riddles, Mr. Raven tells him: " 'What you call riddles are truths, and seem riddles

because you are not true. . . . And you must answer the riddles.
. . . They will go on asking themselves until you understand
yourself. The universe is a riddle trying to get out, and you are
holding your door hard against it.' " On another occasion he tells
Vane: " '. . . no man understands anything; when he knows he
does not understand, that is his first tottering step — not toward
understanding, but toward the capability of one day understanding' "; and on still another occasion he says: " '. . . indeed the
business of the universe is to make such a fool of you that you
will know yourself for one, and so begin to be wise!' " The
puzzling character of the universe has behind it the divine intention of creating humility in man and preparing him for an
eventual revelation of its true nature. When man in his inner
being is spiritually mature enough to understand it, he will.

THE BAGS AND THE LITTLE ONES

Of especial interest in MacDonald's presentation of the theme
of becoming are the Bags and the Little Ones, or Lovers. The
latter apparently represent people of particularly tender sensibility and naiveté whose spiritual life is in its infancy. They owe
their birth to being snatched from Bulika by the white leopardess
(sorrow, as we shall see later), who leaves them in a wood
(spiritual confusion, as in Dante); there they are found by Lona
(redeeming love), who takes them in her charge. But they lack
the water they need to grow into maturity.

Lilith has stolen the water from the surface of their land; what
remains runs underground, and seems inaccessible. The water
image, similar to that in *Phantastes,* seems to suggest life itself:
the life essential. MacDonald is, I think, drawing upon the biblical
image of Living Water: the life of God that Scripture indicates
He bestows upon those who believe. In the conclusion of *Lilith*,
"the river of the water of life" flows from around the throne of
the "Ancient of Days."[7] If Vane had stayed with the Little Ones

7Cf. Ezekiel 47 and John 4:10-15.

and dug them wells, Mr. Raven tells him, he would have helped them. After Vane and his party have arisen from their sleep and are journeying toward God, they find wide rivers of water restored to the land's surface. "Instinctively" the Little Ones plunge in and swim, and then for the first time they see "the glory of God in the limpid flow of water." A combination of Lilith's theft, Vane's misconceived philanthropy, and the Little Ones' own irresponsible attitudes has kept them from at least glimpsing this vision earlier, and receiving its life-giving effects.

The Little Ones' spirit of abandon and naiveté, however, does not render them immune from the danger of retrogession. If they grow apathetic and withdraw from the group, beginning to eat the fruit of the Bags, they rapidly start to become Bags. The Bags are giant creatures who are spiritually dull, cruel, and self-satisfied. Conceptually they are related to the wooden men without joints and sense perception that the knight met and defeated in *Phantastes*. Both groups are insensitive and stupid, with a very narrow and circumscribed view of existence, and do harm to the innocent good.

One feels that here again MacDonald has one eye upon the contemporary religious scene and is commenting upon the moral and spiritual state of two types of people. The Little Ones are those who have not been taught enough to be familiar with religious truth, and are therefore spiritually weak and in danger of falling away. The Bags are those who have turned away from simple and sincere religious interests and whose lives are therefore crass and dull. The latter threaten the former, particularly when they adopt hypocritical roles. MacDonald's fiction abounds with examples.[8]

But MacDonald is not pessimistic about the outcome of the conflict between the two. Mara tells Vane that in the library of the palace at Bulika there is a manuscript in which it is written that " 'after the Lovers have gone through great troubles and

[8]E.g., Robert Bruce, the merchant, in *Alec Forbes of Howglen*, Rev. Slater in *Sir Gibbie*, and, in the fairy tales, the giant in "The Giant's Heart."

learned their own name, they will fill the land, and make the giants their slaves.' " Before the Lovers, or Little Ones, leave for the seige of Bulika, they gain courage to throw off the yoke of the giants and drive them out of their land. The aggressiveness of the Little Ones in finally opposing the giants and in attacking Bulika may seem somewhat out of character with the Christian virtues of meekness, lowliness, and patience that they first possess and that MacDonald emphasizes elsewhere.[9] But they *are* "lovers" and their action may be meant to symbolize the power of love to overcome evil. Perhaps it is the necessity for the Christian to wage spiritual warfare — what Paul speaks of in Ephesians chapter six — that MacDonald has in mind. In any case, their behavior is effective: they do capture Lilith.

THE BULIKANS

Similar to the Bags are the inhabitants of Bulika. They are pictured as victims of Lilith, whose cravings for power subdued them and keep them in terror, but they have developed a loyalty to her and a pride in their city. Mara describes them to Vane as a "prosperous" and " 'self-satisfied people — good at bargaining and buying, good at selling and cheating . . . despising everyone they get the better of. . . . The depth of their worthlessness and height of their vainglory no one can understand who has not been there to see, who has not learned to know the miserable misgoverned and self-deceived creatures.' " No incident shows them pursuing their mercantile interests, but their inhumane attitudes toward Vane when they discover him inside their city show their low state of spiritual development.

In his writings MacDonald consistently directs particular scorn toward characters who are enslaved to money and who display the consequent vices, such as covetousness and greed. In the novel *Thomas Wingfold, Curate,* MacDonald has one of the characters, Joseph Polwarth, recite a prose poem depicting the ideal

[9]See, for instance, "The Heirs of Heaven and Earth," *HG.*

city. The means of commerce and the handling of supply and
demand presented in harmony with Christian principles stand
in strong contrast to the evils of this commercial "Babylon,"
Bulika.[10] The evil of Bulika, however, is primarily presented
rhetorically, not dramatically.

THE PRESENTATION OF EVIL

Of noteworthy interest in *Lilith* are the effects which Mac-
Donald's doctrine of evil have upon his fictional world. We have
noted above, particularly in our discussion of *At the Back of the
North Wind,* that MacDonald views evil — the evil of seemingly
adverse circumstances and events in an individual's experience —
as sacramental, good in terrible disguise. But the evil of spiritually
destructive attitudes is quite another thing, as he makes clear in
his sermons. These attitudes, with their consequent actions, bring
on a spiritual retrogression that has horrendous effects on the
individual, both here and in the nether world. Such evil is the
one great nightmare of the universe, enthralling large segments
of mankind, as the Bulikan society suggests. Nevertheless, because
MacDonald sees evil as negation, it is by its very nature self-
destroying. The triumph of good is a necessity arising from the
very nature of both good and evil. Evil will one day be seen to
have brought about a far greater good than would have been
possible by any other means.[11]

The imaginative presentation of these ideas in *Lilith* tends to
be disappointing, because neither evil characters nor wrong decisions have much dramatic force or convincing power. The two

[10]MacDonald might have chosen this name to suggest "like bulk," which
would underline his attitude toward the material preoccupations of the
city's inhabitants. The initial "B" also recalls Babylon, the epitome of the
secular world in the book of Revelation. Reis conjectures that the name is
"perhaps *bull* plus *ikon,* a pagan idol, suggesting something like Babylon"
(p. 97).

[11]For MacDonald's view of the nature of evil, see "The Voice of Job",
US II.

prominent evil personages are Lilith and the Shadow. The former, who is responsible for the evil attitudes of Bulikans and the thwarted growth of the Little Ones — and consequently of the existence of the Bags — ceases to be evil with comparatively little actual suffering when she submits to sleep in Eve's charnel house. The Shadow, who seems to be a depiction of Satan, does not appear actively nefarious; he seems rather to haunt the streets of Bulika to the great danger of no one. And he, too, eventually lies down and sleeps the sleep that purifies. Thus the only final consequences of these long careers in evil is that the two will be the "last to wake in the morning of the universe."

But perhaps MacDonald's most serious failure to give convincing dramatic expression to his view of the nature of evil occurs in the experiences of Vane himself, when he disobeys Mr. Raven's explicit command that he sleep in Eve's house before he attempts to help the Little Ones. In his meeting with Mr. Raven after his initial experience with Lilith, Vane promises that he will go with him immediately to sleep. Then Vane sees the horse which will be his for his task after he awakes, and in defiance of the raven and disregard of his newly given promise, he mounts the horse and starts to ride away toward the land of the Little Ones. The raven croaks: " '. . . think what you are doing! Twice already has evil befallen you — once from fear, and once from heedlessness: breach of word is far worse; it is a crime.' " When Vane refuses to be dissuaded even though Mr. Raven tells him he will do the Little Ones "other than good" if he goes through with his intention, Mr. Raven then exclaims: " 'Go, then, foolish boy! . . . Take the horse, and ride to failure! May it be to humility!' "

Vane has already suffered the evil consequences of his previous mistakes: first, in the terror and physical torture that he underwent in the Evil Wood and in the captivity of the Bags; and second, in the debilitating leech bites and threat of falling under Lilith's power as her lover-cohort. As the raven points out, these experiences resulted from his fear of sleeping in Eve's house and his neglect to heed the warning he was given not to trust anyone who had deceived him. These instances of evil have been comparatively plausible and, one feels, appropriate to the weaknesses or mistakes to be corrected. Thus, given Vane's present presumptuous actions and the force of Mr. Raven's dire warning, one rightly expects that Vane will now be recompensed with an evil equal to his foolhardiness.

But not so. Vane marshalls the Little Ones on an expedition to Bulika. It is successful, inasmuch as Lilith is captured and delivered to Mara's house, and eventually to Adam's. The most serious cost of the seige is that Lona is killed, but her death is in no sense tragic, because it initiates the sleep that is necessary for her glorification. She is taken to Adam and Eve's "cemetery" where she is laid, and later she awakes with Vane and others at the "morning of the universe." Vane's grief is for no more than the loss of her companionship for the interim between her death and his lying down to sleep himself. In this period, Vane develops the humility that Mr. Raven predicted would be the consequence of Vane's "failure" (in what sense?): he asks forgiveness for his rashness and obediently fulfills the task assigned him. One must observe again, in fairness to MacDonald, that punitive suffering for wrongdoing is foreign to his system of belief; suffering for sin is exclusively corrective. But even so, to be convincing, corrective experience should have a weight that more nearly matches that of the mistake. It is difficult to see these consequences as being equal to the seriousness of Vane's disobedience.

The most satisfying scenes dealing with the nature and consequences of evil to the individual are those picturing the futile activities and empty conversations of the shades. These scenes occur before Vane meets Lilith — who, one later learns, oversees each scene. The first occurs as Vane passes through the Evil Wood, the place where, Mr. Raven has told him, those who refuse to sleep are burying their dead. At night Vane sees, as in a dream, "gathering multitudes" break out into tumultuous battle, filling the air with their vociferous cries. It is a battle of opposing opinions and ideological systems:

> *... phantom-throats swelled the deafening tumult with the war cry of every opinion, bad or good, that had bred strife, injustice, cruelty in any world. The holiest words went with the most hating blow. Lie-distorted truths flew hurtling in the wind. . . . Every moment someone would turn against his comrades, and fight more wildly than before,* The Truth! The Truth! *still his cry.*

Thus MacDonald, who would ally himself with no system, scorns the sectarian mentality that so vehemently expends its energies in futile clashes with those of opposing opinions. "None stooped to comfort the fallen, or stepped wide to spare him," Vane observes, pointing up the utter lack of humane concern that characterizes such sectarian feuds. That they are particularly characteristic of these beings who are extremely low on the scale of becoming is another indication of MacDonald's low opinion of all such activity.

Even so, these warriors are "centuries ahead" of the two grotesque shades whose conversation Vane overhears after he leaves Mara's cottage on the way to Bulika. They are a man and his wife from the leisured aristocracy whose earthly lives were characterized by sensuality and slavish conformity to the rigid and empty social standards of the upper-class world. Amid their bickering and petty contentions, they are forced to help one another: the "lord" cannot walk unless his wife binds the joints of his skeletal knee. The raven explains their situation to Vane:

> *"My lord used to regard my lady as a worthless encumbrance, for he was tired of her beauty and had spent her money; now he needs her to cobble his joints for him! These changes have roots of hope in them. Besides, they cannot now get far away from each other, and they see none else of their own kind: they must at last grow weary of their mutual repugnance, and begin to love one another! for love, not hate, is deepest in what Love 'loved into being.' "*

These skeletons, then, are nearing the turning point in their moral experience. It will occur when one of them extends himself, ever so slightly, for the other. Later in the fantasy, when the army of Little Ones is taking the captive Lilith to Mara's house, this lord and lady again appear. Their appreciation of the attention that the war party gives them in passing indicates that they have turned, repenting their former attitudes, and have begun their long spiritual trek toward fullness of being.

Vane first meets this couple immediately after he has seen a huge crowd of shades. This multitude completes MacDonald's depiction of hell — for so Mr. Raven identifies the place to Vane. They are "gorgeously dressed men and gracefully robed women" who "in dance after dance . . . vaguely embodied the story of life, its meetings, its passions, its parting." As Vane observes them he wonders at the grotesquerie of their appearance: every face is skeletal, every eye-socket is filled with a "lidless living eye" that symbolizes their life-in-death existence. Vane speculates: "Did they know each how they appeared to the others — a death with living eyes? Had they used their faces, not for communication, . . . but to appear what they wished to appear, and conceal what they were? and, having made their faces masks, were they therefore deprived of those masks, and condemned to go without faces until they repented?" In a fashion somewhat similar to Dante's presentation of the damned in the *Inferno,* in which a sinner's condition and punishment are appropriate to specific sins committed on earth, MacDonald depicts those who indulged in various forms of hypocrisy, to him one of the most prevalent and damning of sins. Yet, rather than being fixed in their condition (as are Dante's sinners), MacDonald's sinners are destined eventually to have an opportunity to repent. His thought demands that this will one day be the case.

The evil that befalls the damned and finally works its own destruction in them, with its accompanying sorrows and sufferings, differs only in degree from that evil that befalls Vane in his own spiritual odyssey. When Mr. Raven warns Vane not to trust any person who once deceived him, Vane asks what will happen if he "forgets" the injunction. " 'Then some evil that is good for you will follow' " is the reply. " 'And if I remember?' " Vane asks. " 'Some evil that is not good for you, will not follow,' " the raven answers. This seems to indicate that Vane can only experience corrective evil. His life is constantly under the protective scrutiny of the moon, which, as in *Phantastes,* signifies the providential protection of God. That Vane sees the moon begin "to descend rolling like the nave of Fortune's wheel bowled by the gods" and disappear beyond the horizon-edge immediately after he has seized the horse and ridden off in disobedience to the raven may indicate the extent to which Vane's defiance affronts Providence itself. Nevertheless, events demonstrate that no harm befalls him except that designed to effect his good.

In MacDonald's thought, God's obligation to care for man is complete, by the very nature of both God and man. He writes in his sermon "The Voice of Job":

> . . . *God owes* himself *to the creature he has made in his image, for so he has made him incapable of living without him. This, his creatures' highest claim upon him, is his divinest gift to them. For the fulfilling of this their claim he has sent his son, that he may himself, the father of him and of us, follow into our hearts. . . . No claim had we to be created: that involves an absurdity; but, being made, we have claims on him who made us: our needs are our claims.*

Man's claims upon God do not spring from any supposed human sufficiency. Man is created with needs he *cannot* supply himself; thus he may depend on God to supply them.[12]

God, therefore, so oversees the events of an individual's experience that they are suited to minister to his inner state. They are designed to work upon whatever attitudes or traits need correcting. As Vane leaves Mara's house, he remarks to himself:

---

[12]Among others, two things follow from these "claims" that sinful man has upon God. First, the good that God would do for wayward man may well appear terrifying, and receiving it may be initially painful, as Curdie's experience with the fire of roses in *The Princess and Curdie* graphically shows. Second, God will most surely satisfy the claim of all men upon Him. It is impossible that God would be satisfied to abandon the "non-elect" to their own destinies, as the Westminster Confession asserts, the harsh declarations of which MacDonald counters in his writing.

"I Wis We War A'Deid!"

"That which is within a man, not that which lies beyond his vision, is the main factor in what is about to befall him: the operation upon him is the event." A stronger confidence in the gracious purposes of God in the affairs of one's life could hardly be expressed.[13]

MARA AND THE LEOPARDESSES

Sorrow, like evil, is corrective. In the midst of the Evil Wood Vane finds lodging for a night in Mara's cottage. Mara is a biblical name meaning "bitter,"[14] and this enigmatic character depicts the sorrow that comes from misfortune and adversity. Mac-Donald places a premium upon this sorrow, an importance he communicates in more than one way. Mara is, first of all, a noble character, with dignity and beauty all her own. Few see her face, but when Vane does he finds it "lovely as a night of stars." To meet her is to encounter sorrow; to see her kind countenance is to be assured of her hidden but gracious purposes. Meeting Vane, she tells him: " 'When you know me, call me by the name that seems to you to fit me. . . . That will tell me what sort you are. People do not often give me the right one. It is well when they do.' " Clearly one's attitude toward misfortune and sorrow in life indicates the true nature of his moral character.

In the fantasy Mara is associated with Psalm 30:5: "Weeping may endure for a night, but joy cometh in the morning." This is why, as she tells Vane, no one sleeps more than one night at a time in her house of sorrows; after the sleeper experiences sorrow, joy soon follows. But to try to avoid this grief, this weeping, or to prevent that of others, is in itself folly. Thus, when Vane and Mr. Raven meet in the midst of Vane's experiences, and Vane suggests to him that he suspects what the Little Ones lack is water, he replies:

[13]MacDonald may have in mind the Psalmists' assured attitudes toward evil found in such passages as Psalm 23:4; 91:9, 10; and 121:7.

[14]Reis, p. 97.

The Harmony Within • George MacDonald

"Of course it is! they have none to cry with!"
"I would gladly have kept them from requiring any for that purpose!"
"No doubt you would —the aim of all stupid philanthropists! Why Mr. Vane, but for the weeping in it, your world would never have become worth saving!"

Here water, which we have already suggested seems to symbolize life of spiritual quality, appears in the form of tears. Sorrow is necessary to this life: it is, it seems; the only element out of which true spiritual life grows. A philanthropy that tries only to alleviate sorrow is of questionable value, because it hinders moral growth and spiritual well-being. These ideas seem to be reinforced symbolically by the incident of the stream flowing from the spotted leopard's paw, the event beginning Chapter Twenty-two. Vane sees the stream first as blood, and then discovers it has become beautiful water. The blood probably suggests suffering; the water, life.

Both Mara and Lilith have a cat, or leopardess self, and both bear a close relation to the Shadow. Vane finds it difficult at first to tell the two apart, beyond the fact that the one leopardess has spots while the other is pure white. He knows that Lilith is the spotted leopardess because its actions are consistent with her character. But he is puzzled at first by the actions of the white leopardess, who is closely associated with the Shadow, frequently seen following at his heels. Vane eventually discovers, however, that the white leopardess means to befriend him. When Vane himself begins to follow the Shadow, she drives him back; when Lilith tries to seduce him, she gives a warning cry; and when he is spending a night alone in the streets, she warms and comforts him. Perhaps MacDonald is showing his reader that, although sorrow is associated with evil, it protects the individual who heeds its warnings from being really harmed by it — that is, sorrow issues in salvation. The spotted leopardess, on the other hand, is truly dangerous. It is this one that inflicts the leech-like bites on Vane in an attack which, if repeated, would have killed him, and whose snatching of children is deadly.

"I Wis We War A'Deid!"

Vane further learns that the white leopardess steals the babies to keep them alive, not to kill them. Also, when the two leopardesses fight, the white has the "greater endurance" and prevails. Clearly, the presence of the white leopardess in Bulika acts as a restraining force, stemming the power and controlling the effects of evil. In this way MacDonald may be symbolically expressing Paul's observation: "For godly grief produces a repentance that leads to salvation and brings no regret, but worldly grief produces death" (II Cor. 7:10).

BIBLICAL SOURCES OF SYMBOLS

One is reminded of a number of Scripture passages as he reads *Lilith,* and many of the book's symbols are similar to Scriptural ones. In addition to the ones already mentioned, these symbols include references to childbearing being the death (and salvation) of Lilith (cf. I Tim. 2:15); new names and knowing one's name (cf. Rev. 2:17); going "in and out" of home (cf. John 10:9); the "dead burying their dead" in the Evil Wood (Matt. 8:22); the shades' comment to Lilith, " 'Thou wilt soon become like unto us' " (Isa. 14:9, 10); "the mirror of the Law of Liberty" into which Lilith looks (cf. Jas. 1:22-25);[15] the Shadow's head under Eve's heel (cf. Gen. 3:15); removing the beam from one's eye (Matt. 7:3-5); and various aspects of the universe at the time of its "morning" (cf. Rev. 21, 22). Two other important symbols whose significance may be defined in terms of biblical passages must be considered more fully: Lilith's dark spot and her closed hand.

[15]Woolf finds this a "confused and confusing" image (*GK*, p. 363), but a comparison of MacDonald's use of this image with its source in James makes the meaning clear enough. Cf.: "Nothing is so pleasant to ordinary human nature as to know itself by its reflection from others. When it turns from these warped and broken mirrors to seek its reflection in the divine thought, then it is redeemed; then it beholds itself in the perfect law of liberty" (*The Marquis of Lossie*, Chapter 2). This suggests Lilith's experience with mirrors throughout the fantasy. The liberty Lilith knows in the end is that higher liberty in goodness that Mara explained to her when she was brought, bound, to her dwelling.

From Lilith's first introduction into the fantasy, she is identified as the woman with the spot on her side. In her struggles
in Mara's cottage just before she is sent a vision of her true self
as God sees her, a worm appears and enters her being through
a spot, now grown quite large. And, one recalls, Lilith is the
leopard with the spots. In Scriptural symbolism, spots suggest
blemishes and are often associated with sin. In Levitical law, for
instance, a sacrifice to God must be without spot. A quotation
from Jeremiah is particularly germane: "Can the Ethiopian change
his skin or the leopard his spots? Then also you can do good
who are accustomed to do evil" (13:23). A spot that quickly
spreads, gangrene, is in the English of the King James Version
called a "canker," which suggests cankerworm. Christ often characterized hell as the place where "their worm does not die, and
the fire is not quenched" (Mark 9:48).

In describing Lilith's spot, MacDonald seems to have all this
in mind, together with his hope for the final salvation of man.
The leopard may not be able to change its spots, but the spots
may change it. The growing spot seems to suggest evil eating like
a canker to the very quick of Lilith's being, destroying all but
her very essence, which then can submit to the sleep that heals
and makes whole. The worm proceeds out of the fire on Mara's
hearth, and is itself described as "white hot, vivid as incan-
descent silver, the live heart of essential fire." As the worm
penetrates into Lilith's being, she has the terrible experience of
"seeing herself." Mara explains:

> "She is far away from us, afar in the hell of her self-consciousness.
> The central fire of the universe is radiating into her the knowledge of
> good and evil, the knowledge of what she is. She sees at last the good
> she is not, the evil she is. She knows that she is herself the fire in
> which she is burning, but she does not know that the Light of Life is
> the heart of that fire."

Apparently MacDonald is thus interpreting Christ's imagery
of worm and fire. The irreducible essence of man is itself like

fire, which is as well the holy nature of God, capable of consuming all that is foreign to it. This scene appears to be a definitive depiction of MacDonald's view of human nature and the meaning of human sinfulness.

The meaning of the symbol of the clenched hand may derive from this same warning Christ gives concerning hell. He admonishes: "And if your hand causes you to sin, cut it off; it is better for you to enter life maimed than with two hands to go to hell . . ." (Mark 9:43). Lilith's left hand has been clenched throughout the story, and becomes the focus of attention in Mara's cottage when it is the final remaining obstacle that keeps her from sleep. She protests that she is unable to open it of her own free will, and finally asks Adam to cut it off. He does, using a sword that brings "healing and not hurt." She then immediately falls asleep.

The clenched hand seems to suggest Lilith's acquisitive nature, her taking and keeping things from others. Her yielding her hand suggests her willingness to restore what she has taken. Vane's burying her severed hand restores water to the land, which recalls her original stealing of the water from the Little Ones. But the principle governing her life has been taking from others what is rightfully theirs in order to have power over them. Mr. Raven describes her to Vane as living "by the blood and lives and souls of men." Her acquisitiveness, so deeply embedded within her that she cannot free herself from it, seems to be the "offending member" from which she must be freed to "enter into life."

SALVATION THROUGH CHILDBEARING

The prophecy that Lilith has feared throughout the story is that she "shall be saved by her childbearing." The manner in which this occurs in the fantasy may be taken to represent MacDonald's view of the meaning of the Old Testament assertion that God in his jealousy visits the iniquities of the fathers (mothers?) upon the children. If God punishes sin, MacDonald insists, it is solely for the sake of destroying the sin and saving the sinner: if God visits suffering upon children for the sake of their parents, it must be necessary for the salvation of both.[16] The pattern of events involving Lilith and Lona illustrates this belief.

As Adam's first wife, Lilith bears him Lona and then, supposing that she had herself created the child, wants Adam to worship her. When he refuses and she flees to become queen of Hell, she begins to suppose that parents lose their immortality in their children, and sets out to destroy Lona (thus epitomizing selfishness). But Lona grows up to become the epitome of love, and the loving child desires the redemption of the parent.

With her army of Little Ones, Lona pursues Lilith to Bulika, and at their meeting runs to embrace her. Lilith kills her daughter: the evil parent suffers in hate, the good child in love. But immediately the Little Ones — offspring, as it were, of Lona's love — overcome Lilith and take her to her "death" in Eve's house. Thus MacDonald seems to suggest that Lilith's sin is visited upon her child to her own salvation. Even Lilith's batself becomes the golden rooster of God, his crow "the cry of a chaos that would be a kingdom" as the party begins to awake from their sanctifying sleep.

[16]See, for instance, Deuteronomy 5:9. On punishment, MacDonald writes: "When a man loathes himself, he has begun to be saved. Punishment tends to this result. Not for its own sake, not as a make-up for sin, not for divine revenge — horrible words — not for any satisfaction to justice, can punishment exist. Punishment is for the sake of amendment and atonement. God is bound by his love to punish sin in order to deliver his creature: he is bound by his justice to destroy sin in his creature" ("Justice," US III). Commenting on Luke 4:16-21, MacDonald says this about vengeance: "The point at which the Lord stops in his reading is suggestive: he closes the book, leaving the words 'and the day of vengeance of our God,' . . . unread: God's vengeance is as holy a thing as his love, yea, is love . . . but, apparently, the Lord would not give the word a place in his announcement of his mission: his hearers would not recognize it as a form of the Father's love, but as vengeance on their enemies, not vengeance on the selfishness of those who would not be their brother's keeper" ("Jesus and His Fellow Townsmen," HG).

PRACTICAL ATONEMENT

Nor was Lona really harmed at Lilith's hands. When Lilith is about to succumb to sleep in Eve's house, Eve tells her: " 'Your own daughter you have but sent into the loveliest sleep, for she was already a long time dead when you slew her. And now Death shall be the atonemaker; you shall sleep together.' " Death to lower selves is prerequisite to all effective altruism; hence, we are told, Lona had previously died. Her spiritual deaths are, of course, phenomena quite distinct from her physical death at Lilith's hands.[17] In Eve's house Lilith's enmities toward Lona will be replaced with loving attitudes as they sleep together, and thus practical atonement will be realized.

This practical atoning for past wrongs is not to be taken as a substitute in MacDonald's thought for the Atonement of Christ. Rather, it is demanded by Christ's death, being the inevitable issue of it. Christ's death brings God and men together by revealing God's love, which offers forgiveness to all men for all sin. The estrangement between God and man thus overcome by God in Christ, all lesser enstrangements between men must be practically obliterated by men themselves. God is concerned with *making* men become righteous — not simply declaring them to be so by imputing righteousness to them — and an essential part of this process is their working to right the wrongs they have commited. Thus after Vane succumbs to sleep (during which he dreams), he recounts: "Then, of a sudden, but not once troubling my conscious bliss, all the wrongs I had ever done, from far beyond my earthly memory down to the present moment, were with me. Fully in every wrong lived the conscious I, confessing, abjuring, lamenting the deed, making atonement with each per-

[17]Failing to allow MacDonald the twofold sense of death as both physical and spiritual, Woolf is quite unhappy with this passage (*GK*, p. 363). That Lona formerly had died to her lower selves is evidenced by her selfless serving of the Little Ones (without such death, MacDonald has told us, philanthropy is ineffective). Sleep in Eve's cemetery — still necessary — follows at the proper time. Lilith had killed Lona physically, which is quite another matter, and she is rightfully to blame for doing so.

son I had injured, hurt, or offended." This scene brings to mind one of MacDonald's favorite texts, words of Christ that recur in his sermons: "Truly, I say to you, you will never get out till you have paid the last penny" (Matt. 5:36).[18]

DREAMING OR AWAKE?

Despite his progress, Vane has not yet reached perfection. He is suddenly beset by doubts: is it not all simply a lovely but deluding dream? " 'Be content for a while not to know surely,' " Father Adam replies. " 'The hour will come, and that ere long, when, being true, thou shalt behold the very truth, and doubt will be for ever dead.' " The essential thing, Father Adam tells Vane, is to never waver in obedience to the truth he knows. " 'Trials yet await thee, heavy, of a nature thou knowest not now,' " he warns. Thus MacDonald conveys imaginatively a feeling for the degree of spiritual development Vane must still undergo to "look Truth in the face."

In his sermons MacDonald presents the end of his vision as full, active, loving fellowship between perfected humanity and the Triune God, but he stops short of attempting to project this imaginatively in *Lilith*.[19] He is careful, rather, to maintain the dynamic sense of movement ever upward into increasingly lovely states of more complete life. " '*The* Life keeps generating ours,' " Lona explains. " '. . . here all is upwardness and love and glad-

[18]Because of this insistence on the practical aspects of atonement, some readers may misunderstand MacDonald's position. He explains: "I believe that Jesus Christ *is* our atonement; that through him we are reconciled to, made one with God. There is not one word in the New Testament about reconciling God to us. . . . It is God who has sacrificed his own Son to us; there was no way else of getting the gift of himself into our hearts. Jesus sacrificed himself to his Father and the children to bring them together — all the love on the side of the Father and the Son, all the selfishness on the side of the children. . . . Who that believes in Jesus does not long to atone to his brother for the injury he has done him?" ("Justice," *US* III). He opposes any theory of the Atonement that leaves man solely the passive recipient of its effects.

[19]See particularly "The Creation in Christ," *US* III.

ness.' " In avoiding the suggestion of stasis that one encounters in Dante's paradise and insisting instead upon continual growth and development, MacDonald manifests his own romantic temperament and reminds us again how much he belongs to the romantic spirit of his age. Vane continues to grow, depicted as experiencing an ever-increasing unity with all things:

> A wondrous change had passed upon the world — or was it not rather that a change more marvellous had taken place in us? . . . Every growing thing showed me, by its shape and colour, its indwelling idea. . . . The world and my being, its life and mine, were one. The microcosm and macrocosm were at length atoned, at length in harmony! I lived in everything; everything entered and lived in me.

The quest for one's home, with which the fantasy began, is nearing fulfillment as Vane's capacity to receive the sacramental energies of the universe becomes more complete. Yet all the while, we are reminded, as Vane's feelings of enstrangement from and bewilderment with the universe are diminishing, his individuality and personhood are growing. He is not losing himself in the All.

The essential sacrament for the continuance of this development seems to be still more lovely dreams; to "awake" to the surface realities of the actual world seems to be a retrogression. Vane is "alone, in the land of dreams." When he wishes himself awake, he suddenly tumbles back into this world, and feels "unspeakable despair." He blames himself because he had fled his dream. Apparently one should, for his spiritual health, maintain the strength of his best dreams, but one cannot always summon them at will. We are again reminded of one of the meanings of Vane's name as we see him futilely attempting to return to Father Adam's realm. Then, we are told, he suddenly awakes on his couch in Eve's house, with Lona by his side, and realizes that he had never lost her. For MacDonald himself, doubts and moods of seeming spiritual emptiness were not an unusual part of his spiritual odyssey. He seems to be suggesting here that although the good dream may not stay in constant focus, it does recur.

Also, the distinctions between states of consciousness imaged by waking and sleeping becomes unimportant, and MacDonald clinches his point that in this upward progression of spiritual development each prior state becomes like a past dream, with each new state being one of more intense consciousness.

At the conclusion of the penultimate chapter, just as Vane and his party are at last approaching the throne of "the Ancient of Days" and in a cloud of glory are lead by a "hand, warm and strong," through a door with a golden lock, Vane suddenly finds himself "alone in his library," and faces again the question, Is it all illusion? But the answer issues from the lips of Hope that, although the dream came from Vane's own "dark self," it was put there by God, by whose integrity it will be realized. He therefore affirms: "But when I wake at last into that life which, as a mother her child, carries this life in its bosom, I shall know that I wake, and shall doubt no more." For this, Vane is content to wait — and, it would seem, so was MacDonald.[20]

EVALUATION

Within MacDonald's system of thought, what Lilith has done all men must do if they are to be saved. The sooner an individual earnestly undertakes to die to his inferior selves, and to nurture his true self, the sooner he comes to spiritual health and growth. For those who will not do so, there are experiences of ever-increasing pain and horror ahead. *Lilith* makes us feel this view of the nature of salvation with an imaginative power wielded by few pieces of literature dealing with man's eternal destiny.

[20]I find no basis in *Lilith* or in MacDonald's writings in general to agree with Woolf's harsh assessment: "Close reading of *Lilith* has convinced me . . . that, despite powerful and occasionally moving passages, it is feeble, ambiguous, and inconsistent in its imagery, full of senile hatreds and re-sentments, and the most violent in its aggressions of all MacDonald's works. The consolations that it professes seem to have lost their meaning for the author himself" (*GK*, p. 332). Reis disagrees, contending that the ending of *Lilith* is consistent with MacDonald's affirmation of both life and death, and with his view that enlightenment in this life is never complete (p. 102).

Nevertheless, the fantasy as a whole is an uneven performance in its final form, and somewhat inferior to *Phantastes*. One cannot help feeling that the original version could have been revised — and that with fewer changes — into a more aesthetically satisfying fantasy than we now have as the authoritative one. The first version is more compact, contains less overt sermonizing, and omits the material that is least well-realized dramatically: Lona, the Little Ones, the Bags, and the entire incident of Vane's disobedience to Adam.[21] MacDonald's actual revision on the whole dilutes the material, and although it is still generally far from allegory (in the sense of a very transparent and mechanical one-to-one relation of meaning to symbol), the final version does take some steps in that direction. Perhaps here is another evidence of MacDonald's romantic temperament: material that stands closest to the original creative vision retains more of the original fire; alterations tend to diminish the flame.

Positively, *Lilith* is to be credited with having generally vivid characters — for myth — and a rather vivid sense of place. MacDonald handles the transitions between the two worlds with expertise. The aura of the dream, with the startling immediacy of its scenes and the peculiar force of its logic, is maintained with admirable consistency. In addition, much of the symbolism serves MacDonald's ideological purposes with an impressive strength. But, these qualities acknowledged, the weaknesses remain to disappoint: the weight of idea that is not integrated with the symbolism, the generally weak dramatic quality, and the lack of convincing moral growth within Vane himself.

[21]Greville opines: "Comparing carefully the two versions, some will think the earlier a better and simpler narrative" (*GMDW*, p. 548). After reading the earlier version, I agree.

CHAPTER SIX

"If You Would But Write
Novels,
Mr. MacDonald"

"This made it more likely that he had seen a true vision; for instead of making common things look commonplace, as a false vision would have done, it had made common things disclose the wonderful that was in them."
—"The Shadows"

*L*ilith was written after MacDonald spent over thirty years detailing his vision of the meaning and significance of life in his many long novels. These novels are all shaped by artistic techniques directly marshaled for the purposes of faith. In a warm and fascinating essay written as a tribute to his father, MacDonald's son Ronald relates this incident:

> Once I asked him why he did not, for a change and variety, write a story of mere human passion and artistic plot. He replied that he would like to write it. I asked him then further whether his highest literary quality was not in a measure injured by what must to many seem the monotony of his theme —referring to the novels alone. He admitted that this was possible; and went on to tell me that, having begun to

"If You Would But Write Novels . . ."

*do his work as a Congregational minister, and having been driven
. . . into giving up that professional pulpit, he was no less impelled
than compelled to use unceasingly the new platform whence he had
found that his voice could carry so far.* [1]

George MacDonald was first of all a Christian; secondly, an artist.
As mentioned in the opening chapter, he turned from writing
fantasy and poetry to writing novels early in his career because
he saw the novel as an effective medium for his message, and
because his publisher urged him to do so.

Had MacDonald's conscience not compelled him to communicate his message very directly to a world he perceived to be
in great need, it is probably safe to say he would have written
few — if any — novels. No doubt he would have made more
contributions to literature in the genre he liked best: fantasy.
But, as it was, he was driven inwardly to make as clear as he
could to as large an audience as possible his understanding of
the relation of Christian truth to human experience. The great
popularity of the novel form — Dickens, Thackeray, and Trollope
were in vogue at the time — must have seemed to offer him the
opportunity he wanted.

Although MacDonald was not unmindful of the distinct literary conventions that govern the separate genres of fantasy and
the realistic novel, in his work the distance between them is less
than one might at first suppose. His writings in both forms
abundantly attest to his strong conviction that a transcendent
reality is so closely related to the world of immediate human
experience that it is also immanent in it. This reality shapes the
spiritual health of man by aiding him to become more morally
upright than he is inclined to be on his own. For man to be good
and do right issues in a mature individuality on a higher plane

[1]"George MacDonald: A Personal Memoir," *From a Northern Window*
(London: Nisbet, 1911), pp. 66-67. This collection of essays lists no editor;
Ian Maclaren writes the first. Reis, also quoting this passage, comments:
"Scarcely any other writer of fiction in any literature so consciously re-
garded his function to be that of a teacher and preacher, rather than to be
that of an entertainer, artist, or money-earner" (p. 47).

of being; for him to do evil is an affront to the true nature of things, behavior that yields spiritual detriment, and, if persisted in, spiritual disintegration. This transcendent reality is presented in the novels in a manner remarkably similar to that of the fantasies: in both, a basic set of images creating the aura of myth forms a substructure of the narrative.

MacDonald must have been attracted to the writing of fantasy at the beginning of his long career because he saw the potential it had to assert the presence of this transcedent yet immanent reality and to explore the moral imperatives it places upon men's lives. When writing novels became for him a necessary alternative to writing fantasies, his purposes in nowise changed; they simply became more directly and explicitly revealed. In the novels moral imperatives and theological insights are considered less symbol-ically, more directly; symbolic embodiment tends to give way to illustration in the lives of characters that appear as real people. But the primary focus is ever upon this elusive yet pervading reality in response to which men's destinies are shaped. Mac-Donald therefore stands in interesting contrast to the more well-known "realist" authors of his day, who were concentrating simply on a more accurate rendering of surface appearances. He also is quite distinct from such a contemporary moralist as George Eliot, whose frequent observations on the moral qualities of her characters serve to reveal character itself and the effects of human behavior upon society, rather than to assert man's immortality and the effects of his behavior upon his eternal destiny. Several other religious novelists, of course, were writing at the same time as MacDonald — Charles Kingsley was one of the more prominent — but few, if any, were as prolific as he, nor do their works seem to achieve as satisfying an integration of the eternal with the temporal as his do.

The novel as a literary type, of course, is an attempt to picture daily human experience. For the imaginative and conscientious Christian author, the novel can become a sort of gauge for measuring the validity of his understanding of Christian truth in its practical reaches. Inadequate views of what Christianity consists of and means clearly offend the discerning reader's sense of reality. Thus the Christian who would write a viable novel is pressured by the very nature of his medium to develop a valid view of the relation of Christian idea to life.

Writing novels did work to keep MacDonald's faith practical and psychologically apt, but this is not to say he wrote great novels. True, the imagined world his novels project is peopled by a startling number of believable characters reacting to experiences in ways that offer deft insight into human behavior. But his plots tend to be conventional, predictable, and melodramatic — a lamentable flaw, given the type of strength his novels do possess.[2]

MacDonald's primary interest in the novels is the reactions of the human mind to a universe which, as we have considered in Chapter Three, is thoroughly sacramental. He took delight in quoting Proverbs 25:2: "It is the glory of God to conceal a thing: but the honor of kings is to search out a matter" (King James Version). In his novels he set himself the task of searching out life and discerning its hidden meanings. In his liberal running commentaries on the action, his insights are generally deft, penetrating, and spiritually provocative; life in its spiritual dimensions is often clarified. But this clarification usually occurs through character reaction, with accompanying commentary, rather than through the overall form of the novel as an authentic portrayal of action.

Another factor contributing to poor quality is the pace at which MacDonald wrote: he was a very energetic author who produced with too great facility an astounding amount of material. Greville lists sixty titles in his bibliography of his father's

[2]I agree in the main with Reis's evaluation of the literary quality of the novels: "No amount of summary . . . can quite convey a number of their essential qualities — the verbosity of style, the flavor of the dialogue, the frequent tediousness, the occasional attainment of high excitement and a verbal grace. MacDonald's frequently excellent material is invariably mixed with, and usually spoiled by, great flaws" (p. 74). He concludes that MacDonald's "appropriate medium" was the symbolic fantasy.

works, and he quotes Ronald as saying that twenty-five of them are novels.[3] It is undeniable that MacDonald did possess the gift of telling a story with verve and intrigue, and portions of his work are artistically admirable. However, both his haste and his fatigue are too often evident.

Archetypal patterns and images form a firm substructure in both MacDonald's fantasies and his novels.[4] To note some of the more outstanding ones offers us a convenient way of seeing all of the novels in relation to each other as well as to the fantasies, and underscores MacDonald's mythic bent.

Several archetypal images are prominent in both the novels and the fantasies: 1) the journey, during which the hero comes into a higher state of moral and spiritual being through a series of related episodes; 2) the sage or prophetess, who gives necessary counsel and advice along the way; 3) the wasteland, through which the hero moves to self-knowledge; 4) the poet, whose powers of vision discern the spiritual world and whose songs move both himself and his listeners toward it; and 5) the ideal woman, who inspires others toward a fuller knowledge of the Ideal. Each of these archetypes bears a particularly close relation to MacDonald's concept of becoming and is used to show how the individual moves toward spiritual maturity.

THE JOURNEY

The image of the journey, which is prominent in the fantasies, appears both literally and symbolically in the novels. In the fantasies, both Anodos and Vane journey through Faerie, experiencing the various adventures of the story. In the novels, the

[3]*GMDW*, p. 563. There are at least this many. Woolf counts 25 (*GK*, p. 4); Reis arrives at 29 (p. 28). The exact number one reaches depends upon whether he includes as novels some of the shorter works MacDonald designated as "tales," and also whether he includes novels intended for adolescents, such as *Gutta Percha Willie: The Working Genius*.

[4]Reis discerns Jungian archetypal patterns in character and plot. See his chapter "The Symbolic Muse."

characters most often make spiritual journeys, so that the archetype of the journey appears as the spiritual road they travel in the process of their moral development. At the beginning of many novels, the hero or heroine has certain character flaws that indicate the distance he or she has to travel on the road to inner maturity. The incidents of the novel then shape and nurture this development, so that by the end the character has arrived at his spiritual destination. *Guild Court* (1868) is a typical example, also illustrative of other characteristics of MacDonald's fiction that we will explore later.

The plot provides the challenges which Thomas Worboise, the hero, must face along his spiritual journey. At the beginning of the novel, Tom is self-centered, ambitious for the "good life" of materialism, indecisive, and rather frivolous, although these traits are not so strong that they alienate the reader from him. He is the son of a shrewd, ambitious lawyer and an invalid mother of strong Evangelical persuasion, and he is working as an apprentice clerk to his father's friend, Mr. Boxall.

Tom is secretly meeting Lucy Burton, an admirable and attractive but poverty-stricken girl who lives with her grandmother Boxall, mother of Tom's employer. His Father, however, wants his son to court one of Boxall's own daughters, Mary, because such an alliance would put him into position to inherit the business. The self-indulgent manner in which Tom behaves toward these girls, both of whom love him, underscores the unpleasant qualities of his character. But, forced to decide between them, he chooses Lucy, in the process rejecting Mary Boxall's affection and falling out of favor with the Boxalls.

Boxall makes out his will with the help of Lawyer Worboise, and in a moment of carelessness, he names his lawyer his beneficiary should his wife and daughters die. Ironically, no sooner does Boxall do this than he and his family are shipwrecked while taking a vacation, and all die in the disaster. Eager for wealth, Worboise presses his claim, even to the extent of cruelly evicting Lucy and her grandmother from their apartment above the premises.

The Harmony Within • George MacDonald

Meanwhile, Tom begins the journey that brings him to spiritual enlightenment. He falls under the influence of a German language instructor who exercises an evil power over him and draws him into gambling. Ruined, dejected, and filled with shame, Tom, having stolen money from the Boxall business to pay a gambling debt, leaves home. His spiritual journey is now symbolized by his physical journey. After a series of adventures in which he rescues a child from drowning and goes to sea as a sailor, he determines to return to Guild Court (a particular small court in London in which small shops and Boxall's business are located and the minor characters live) and ask Lucy's forgiveness.

Doing so, he comes into contact with a Mr. Fuller, an unconventional clergyman who conducts his own nightly church and is identified as being somewhat "Broad Church" in his theology. Mr. Fuller convinces Tom of the necessity of making restitution to those whom he has wronged. Tom does so with admirable courage, his experiences having brought him to his senses, and Lucy is joyously reconciled with him. In the end, Tom is instrumental in proving that since the Boxall family did not all die at the same time (a daughter survived her parents for a short time), the business in question cannot legally go to his father. He is even reconciled with his father, who comes to admire him for his courage and determination.

When in utter dejection Tom has his conversation with Mr. Fuller, the clergyman philosophizes about Tom's past experiences in a manner that reveals MacDonald's intention in presenting the spiritual journey:

> *"You are more honorable now than you were before. Then you were capable of the crime; now, I trust, you are not. It was far better that, seeing your character was such that you could do it, you should thus be humbled by disgracing yourself, than that you should have gone on holding up a proud head in the world, with such a deceitful hollow of weakness in your heart. It is the kindest thing God can do for his children, sometimes, to let them fall in the mire. You would not hold by your Father's hand; you struggled to pull it away; he let it go, and*

"If You Would But Write Novels . . ."

there you lay. Now that you stretch forth the hand to him again, he will take you, and clean, not your garments only, but your heart, and soul, and consciousness."

The journey with its harsh experiences is necessary, because it produces virtue. The pain and disgrace that are inevitable upon the journey — in short, all external evils — are justified because they are intended to humble and enlighten the sufferer. They are meted out by a loving Father who wants to chastise His child in order to turn him to righteousness. Wearied by the episodes of the journey, the defeated individual turns in his weakness to God, who both renews him and, in the future, responds to his obedience by giving him the power to grow. Thus the journey image accomplishes the same ends in the novels as it does in the fantasies.

An interesting variation of the journey motif in MacDonald's novels occurs when he traces the growth of children to both physical and spiritual maturity. In an earlier novel, *Alec Forbes of Howglen* (1865) — which remains in many ways the most delightful of the novels — MacDonald discovered his ability to draw children convincingly. Apparently he also discovered in this novel that tracing the physical growth of an individual, particularly as he undergoes hardships in childhood, can be a fitting and helpful corollary of spiritual development. In fact, many of MacDonald's novels may be classed as *Bildungsroman*: the journey image acquires the dimension of traveling through life toward adulthood as well as traveling through adult experience toward spiritual maturity.

Little Annie Anderson in *Alec Forbes of Howglen* is a convincing and memorable character. An unwanted orphan, she lives in the deprived and niggardly atmosphere of the home of her "benefactor," Robert Bruce, a skinflint grocer. The scene of Annie in her barren garret room at night, deathly frightened by the rats and crying out in prayer, " 'O God, tak care o' me frae the rottans,' " makes a lasting impression upon the reader. In its vivid and pathetic portrayal it is not unlike a passage from Dickens.

The Harmony Within • George MacDonald

As a child Annie deeply admires Alec Forbes, slightly older than she. This admiration blossoms into a worshipful love as he protects her from bullying schoolmates and a tyrannical schoolmaster. Annie grows toward spiritual maturity early in her life, her nature being purged of its dross by unusually severe — but convincing — childhood hardships. Alec, however, must go off to college, start drinking, visit a brothel, and finally go to sea before he realizes how lost he is. He then undergoes a type of conversion that brings him to his senses and prompts his return to home and Annie. This version of the journey archetype later becomes the pattern for several of MacDonald's more successful novels, such as *Robert Falconer, Wilfrid Cumbermede,* and *Sir Gibbie.*

In many of the novels the chief deterrent to a successful journey toward spiritual maturity is contact with false ideas about God's character and manner of working in the world, particularly those fostered by the mean and narrow popular versions of Calvinist doctrines. Many heroes are genuinely perplexed by the doctrines preached by dissenting Evangelical groups. A case in point is the consternation little Annie Anderson feels when she attends the "missionar-kirk" and hears a sermon on the doctrine of election. The scenes in *Malcolm* of the revival meeting in a cave present another travesty of true religious experience: the congregation is seized by fits of emotional frenzy. MacDonald's sense of indignation at the error and vulgarity of such religious expressions is, as one can readily imagine, very strong. He distinguishes between them and his sense of the truth with scathing rebuke.

Many of his portraits of Evangelical believers enslaved to rigid Calvinist doctrines are memorable. Mrs. Worboise, Tom's mother in *Guild Court,* is a good study of the morally despicable attitudes that such a commitment can generate. She is an invalid, constantly ministered to by Mr. Simon, a dissenting minister; together the two of them keep her husband and almost keep Tom from entering the kingdom of heaven. MacDonald describes them caustically:

"If You Would But Write Novels . . ."

> She and her priest belonged to a class more numerous than many of
> my readers would easily believe, a great part of whose religion consists
> in arrogating to themselves exclusive privileges and another great part
> in defending their supposed rights from the intrusion of others. The
> thing does not look such to them, of course, but the repulsiveness of
> their behaviour to those who cannot use the same religious phrases,
> indicating the non-adoption of their particular creed, compels others
> so to conclude concerning their religion. . . . Alas for that people! whose
> god is paltry, shallow-minded and full of party spirit; who sticks to a
> thing because he has said it, accepts a man because of his assent, and
> condemns him because of his opinions. . . .

Mrs. Worboise has a compulsive desire to save her son's soul, a
wish that he undergo a conversion according to the exact steps
she would prescribe. But her obsession only oppresses Tom, alien-
ating him from her and keeping him from a true experience
of God.

Mr. Fuller, the maverick clergyman, helps Tom develop a genuine knowledge of God by articulating MacDonald's idea about
approaching God in truth. Tom is told he must first of all make
restitution for the wrongs he has done and then exercise an
obedient faith: " 'You must give yourself up to the obedience of
his Son entirely and utterly, leaving your salvation to him, troubling yourself nothing about that, but ever seeking to see things
as he sees them, and to do things as he would have them done.
And for this purpose you must study your New Testament in
particular . . . !' " This effort to bring one's view of life into
conformity with God's perspective and will is clearly distinct
from a more narrowly prescribed insistence upon accepting a
"plan of salvation" derived from a mechanical handling of biblical
"proof texts" and involving strongly emotional conversion.

Nevertheless, although MacDonald's opposition to what he
views as perversions of true Christian thought at times appears
to be labored, he also pays large tribute to those staunch characters, particularly Scottish, whose rigid Evangelical commitment
to stern Calvinist doctrine makes them Christians of sterling

virtue. Old Thomas Crann in *Alec Forbes of Howglen* and Mrs. Falconer, Robert's devout grandmother in *Robert Falconer,* are two good examples of such admirable characters. MacDonald muses in *Malcolm,* "Calvinism itself has produced as loving children as abject slaves, with a good many between partaking of the character of both kinds," and he does make an objective attempt to draw both kinds of believers in his works. But those characters who help others to the way of righteousness do so because of their active obedience to Christ's presence. They are motivated by the goodness that this obedience alone generates — not by their particular sectarian alliances or by any self-generated zeal simply to persuade others to adopt their view of religious experience.

THE SAGE

Sage or prophetess figures are to be found in every novel. They offer moral and spiritual instruction that enables the seeker to find himself and to embark on the road to spiritual development. These figures tend to be female in the fantasies — recall, for instance, Mara in *Lilith* and the woman in the cottage with four doors in *Phantastes* — but are generally male in the novels. One can only speculate that this is an unconscious result of Mac-Donald's view of woman and the reality of the fantasy world. Woman stands nearer to the Ideal than man, and the fantasy world stands nearer to the Ideal than does the world of the novel; hence, in the dream world of fantasy women are more suited to giving direction toward the Ideal than men. But in the novels men are often father figures, human surrogates for God the Father, attesting to MacDonald's conviction that fatherhood is at the very heart of the universe. Their approach to the enigmas of life is invariably a carefully reasoned, tightly logical one, unlike the brief, penetrating, authoritative intuitions of women.

MacDonald generally succeeds in drawing these father figures convincingly, but occasionally they are flat and wooden. An example is Mr. Walton, the clergyman whose experiences are detailed in *Annals of a Quiet Neighbourhood* (1867) and its two sequels, *The Seaboard Parish* (1868) and *The Vicar's Daughter* (1872). These novels are among MacDonald's poorest, lapsing as they do into long sermons illustrated by events that too often challenge one's sense of reality.[5]

Some four years after finishing these chronicles of Mr. Walton's experiences, MacDonald returned to the development of the sage as hero in *Thomas Wingfold, Curate* (1876), and performed his task appreciably better. Wingfold is introduced as a curate who is far from being a paragon of spiritual wisdom and ministry: he is a man of typically professional attitudes who maintains his charge in a leisurely and undistinguished way. At the novel's beginning he is startled when an amiable atheist forces him to admit that he wears the cloth in the Church of England simply as a convenient means of livelihood — that he really neither believes nor disbelieves the doctrines of the church which he purports to serve. Wingfold comes alive to the reader as he responds to this realization; an honest man, he endures intense self-searching and inner turmoil to discover and define his beliefs, all the while continuing to function as clergyman. One is compelled to sympathize with Wingfold, to feel with him the awkwardness of his position, and to follow the logical processes whereby a strong apology for MacDonald's own version of Christian doctrines evolves in Wingfold's mind.

In finding himself and his faith, Wingfold is helped immeasurably by Joseph Polwarth, a misshapen dwarf who works as a gatekeeper for the large English estate of the parish. Living in humility and poverty with his crippled niece, he perceives the marrow of life in its spiritual aspects, and he quietly helps all

[5]The fact that both Greville (*GMDW*, p. 154) and Bulloch (p. 688) observe that *Annals of a Quiet Neighbourhood* was praised by many readers as being MacDonald's best novel gives an interesting clue to the literary taste and desires of his reading public. More curious yet is the statement of Ronald, whose literary sensibilities appear to be reasonably sharp, that this novel ranks above all his father's other English novels and with the best of the Scottish (*From a Northern Window*, p. 98).

who seek him out for his sympathetic counsels. In his wisdom, he is typical of a long list of such figures in the novels, true sages of great moral and spiritual insight who stand outside the conventional Christian ministry. They may be laymen, like Polwarth; schoolmasters, like Mr. Graham in *Malcolm* and *The Marquis of Lossie;* unconventional and independent ministers, like Mr. Fuller of *Guild Court;* or simply ideal fathers, such as David Elginbrod in *David Elginbrod* and Cosmo Warlock, Sr., in *Warlock O'Glenwarlock.* All are father figures, functioning as surrogates of the Heavenly Father, to whom they point, and whose mercy and compassionate understanding their attitudes exemplify.

Despite this very great dramatic burden resting upon them, many of these characters are remarkably less stereotyped and mechanical than their function, in the hands of most novelists, would force them to be. One large difficulty, which ensnares most novelists as they attempt to depict characters of unique goodness, is that a character tends to lose his individuality and hence his interest for the reader in direct proportion to his identification with the Good. Distinct personality traits are invariably diminished, if not lost. But MacDonald believed deeply that God has made each man a unique individual, who can worship God and serve Him in a way no one else can, and that the individual's growth toward spiritual maturity develops, rather than diminishes, this individual uniqueness.[6]

Here is one of many instances, then, in which MacDonald's art is directly shaped by his convictions. Most novelists have less difficulty drawing evil characters than they do good characters; they use evil traits to flesh out and distinguish evil characters, but they tend to see the personalities of the good characters as diluted by goodness. MacDonald has just the opposite difficulty: his good characters are impressively individualistic, whereas his evil characters — such as Beauchamp in *Alec Forbes of Howglen* —

[6]See "The New Name," *US* I.
[7]See Lewis, *Anthology*, p. 18: "One rare, and all but unique, merit these novels must be allowed. The 'good' characters are always the best and most convincing. His saints live; his villains are stagey."

are all of a type.[7] This reversal occurred at least partly because MacDonald saw evil as creating a conformity among men that robs them of their distinct individual traits. His success with good characters is also a result of his intensely earnest conviction that he had valid insights into the perennial enigmas of life. The sages in his works understand these enigmas, having themselves grappled successfully with their own personal problems. Therefore, they are able to empathize humbly and compassionately with the heroes in spiritual crises.

For these reasons, MacDonald succeeds in creating in the novels an impressive gallery of characters of great virtue and genuine goodness that are both distinct from each other and convincing in their own right. Their prior interaction with evil and their decisions to resist it have made them free individuals in the best sense of the word.

THE WASTELAND

The decisions of these characters were made during stressful periods in their lives. The wastelands of the fantasies, through which Anodos and Vane both journey to attain spiritual knowledge and development, take a different form in the novels: they are periods of difficult circumstance which the characters who need spiritual development must necessarily face. The wasteland experience is, in the fantasies, an inevitable part of the journey, and, in the novels, the context necessary for spiritual illumination.

These spiritual wastelands take many forms. They may involve a period of sickness, as they do for Juliet Meredith in *Paul Faber, Surgeon,* and Euphra Cameron in *David Elginbrod;* a traumatic discovery, such as Lady Florimel's discovery that she is indeed Malcolm's sister in *The Marquis of Lossie;* or rigorous experiences that transpire "offstage," like the seagoing adventures of Thomas Worboise in *Guild Court.* In *Phantastes,* Anodos falls from the Fairy Palace into a wasteland because of his persistent sensual lusts, and in *Lilith* Vane enters a wasteland as a consequence of disobeying Mr. Raven. The characters in the novels enter their wastelands because they persist in indulging similar vices, generally

marked by an undue self-esteem and a general sense of independence from God.

In these wasteland experiences the hero's soul is loosed from
all its conventional ties and confidences, his pride is destroyed,
and his illusions of self-sufficiency burst. He then discovers himself to be utterly dependent upon the basic spiritual force that
sustains life when all its apparent underpinnings are seen to be
useless. He is often freed from these attitudes and false securities
by events that would normally be considered misfortunes or evil
occurrences. In a manner that we have already discussed,
MacDonald argues in the novels that such external evils are
disguised blessings, intended by the Heavenly Father to bring the
individual to a right orientation to both life and God. These
misfortunes penetrate the facades of false selves and enable the
individual to discover his true self, a spiritual process portrayed
with vivid symbolism in the scene in *Lilith* discussed above. It
depicts the growing spot on Lilith's side and the accompanying
worm eating to the very essence of her being, the divine spark
of life. When the evil is destroyed, this spark can begin to glow
and will soon flame; it is, in short, the image of God within the
soul. As the individual comes to acknowledge his dependence
upon the divine, he is cleansed of his past and, thus renewed,
begins his growth toward spiritual maturity.

THE POET

Another archetypal figure that merits attention is that of the
poet. He does not appear as unfailingly in MacDonald's works
as the other basic images listed above, but he recurs often enough
to capture one's attention. These poets provoke a further comparison to the fantasies, particularly *Phantastes,* in which poems
have great moral and spiritual power. As we will note in our
final chapter, MacDonald's esteem of the poet is derived from
the role that Novalis, the German poet and writer of fantasy,
defines in his tale *Heinrich von Ofterdingen:* the poet has great
insight into the world of the spirit, and can snatch men away

from the familiar present and transport them into that higher region. The world of MacDonald's fantasies is just such a world, and the role of the poet there is to express still deeper insight into the nature of human experience of its ultimate implications.

In the novels, the poet arouses his own spirit and often the spirit of certain sensitive listeners to an awareness of the spiritual world beyond the material world, and he stimulates desire toward it. A good example of the ideal poet in the novels is Donal Grant, the youthful peasant poet in *Sir Gibbie* and *Donal Grant*. He has learned from reading the poetry of Robert Burns something of the poetic power resident in his Scottish language, and Gibbie's spirit feeds upon his rustic ballads while the two tend the cattle on the Scottish hillsides. MacDonald remarks about the function of poetry: "Its true end is to help first the man who makes it along the path to the truth: help for other people may or may not be in it. . . ." Poetry is thus a primary help to the imaginative individual in his pursuit of the truth.

Sir Gibbie is a novel of great charm and, I think, one that possesses an impressive quantity of what C. S. Lewis referred to as "holiness." (See the opening remarks from Lewis's *The Great Divorce* in the Introduction.) In its make-up it is more similar to the fantasies than is the average McDonald novel. The main character, Gibbie, is "one of those few elect natures to whom obedience is a delight — a creature so different from the vulgar that they have but one tentacle they can reach such with — that of contempt." As such he seems suprahuman. Through him MacDonald is imaginatively creating the ideal nature and showing its growth into adulthood.

In his aspirations, his naiveté, and his earnest self-giving for others, Gibbie stands nearer the ideal than is humanly possible, but he is at the same time a delightful creation. MacDonald's power to make goodness interesting is nicely exercised here, and this novel serves as a good introduction to all the novels for the beginning reader. Being freer from the limitations that realistic considerations impose on MacDonald's intentions, *Sir Gibbie* offers one opportunity to study more fully these intentions in their purer form.

An invariable trait of MacDonald's potential saints is that they have a poetic sensibility which makes them either poets themselves or lovers of poetry. Donal's songs help Gibbie, who is already "in the kingdom of heaven," though Donal himself has yet to suffer before his entrance. Donal's poems with their spiritual power combine with Janet's reading of Scripture (she is a godly old Scottish woman, one of the few female sages in the novels) to arouse Gibbie's spirit to reach upward after the divine, thus developing his true self.

WOMAN AND THE IDEAL

In addition to receiving help from the sage and the poet, the hero is aided on his spiritual journey by the love of woman. In the last chapter of *Guild Court,* MacDonald muses upon Thomas Worboise's spiritual journey: "The chief aid which Thomas had in this spiritual growth, next to an honest endeavor to do the work of the day and the hour, and his love to Lucy, was the instruction of Mr. Fuller." In this way he ranks these experiences according to their contribution to spiritual growth: next in importance to personal obedience to God, and above that of the spiritual sage, is love of woman. The novels amply illustrate MacDonald's thoughts about how love of woman affects the spirit of man.

The function of young women in the novels also bears close resemblance to that of the marble lady in *Phantastes* and that of Lona in *Lilith.* But in the novels MacDonald does not dwell upon his distinctions between pure attraction and base lust as he did in *Phantastes.* Apparently Victorian taste could cope with that theme presented in fantasy but would not tolerate it in the more realistic world of the novel. The young women in the novels are pure in heart and noble in ideals, and have a large sensitivity for spiritual values. Man's attraction for woman is generally morally

"If You Would But Write Novels . . ."

pure and acts as a constant inspiration toward the good and a deterrent from the base, giving him incentive to become worthy of her.[8]

In *Paul Faber, Surgeon* (1879), which MacDonald thought was his best novel, he explores quite thoroughly the spiritual effects of love upon both man and woman. The novel offers the possibility that each partner in marriage can function as the other's savior.

Paul Faber is an atheistic doctor, admirable for his honest bearing and humanitarian deeds, living in the same town in which Thomas Wingfold is the curate; in fact, the story is a sequel to the novel about Wingfold. Faber falls in love with one of his patients, Juliet Meredith, a woman who is not a Christian believer but a vague idealist who opposes Faber's rationalism and empiricism. She thus stands nearer to the kingdom of heaven than he. During their courtship MacDonald philosophizes:

> *Was he in love with her? . . . The Maker of men alone understands his awful mystery between the man and the woman. But without it, frightful indeed as are some of its results, assuredly the world he has made would burst its binding rings and fly asunder in shards, leaving his spirit nothing to enter, no time to work his lovely will. . . . Will any man who has ever cast more than a glance into the mysteries of being, dare think himself sufficient to the ruling of his nature? . . . Come thou, holy Love, father of my spirit . . . possess me utterly, for thou art more me than I am myself. Rule thou. . . . And ye, women . . . be the saviours of men, and neither their torment nor their prey!*

[8]MacDonald's view of the effect of the love of woman upon man — which of course, may be traced back to Dante — bears interesting resemblance to that of Tennyson in "Guinevere" of *Idylls of the King:*

> . . . for indeed I knew
> Of no more subtle master under heaven
> Than is the maiden passion for a maid,
> Not only to keep down the base in man,
> But teach high thought, and amiable words
> And courtliness, and the desire of fame,
> And love of truth, and all that makes a man. (Ll. 474-80)

In the story, Juliet first has the opportunity to be Faber's savior, his guide to truth, not by virtue of any Christian commitment on her part but simply by her role as wife. Like man in general, Faber is not himself capable of ruling his nature without God's help. The experience of love will offer him the possibility of redemption, for it is the immediate expression in his life of God's creative power, ready to be expended to make him the man he is not yet. Juliet's responsibility is awesome, for she must neither torment him by not returning his love, nor allow him simply to use her to satiate his lust; rather, she must be ideally the channel of God's creative power flowing toward him.

But Juliet is not as qualified for this role as she should be. After Faber's ardent courtship overcomes her inexplicable hesitations, she marries him, and then both Faber and reader discover why she had hesitated: she had been intimate with another man prior to their wedding. This gives Faber the opportunity to be Juliet's savior. Had he himself been the ideal man, he would have fully forgiven her when she confesses to him in utter contrition, and thus would have helped her to become the better person she longs to be. Instead, Faber sees himself as having been duped, sold, married to a slut, and he utterly rejects her, all her love and genuine goodness notwithstanding. In complete dejection, Juliet goes into hiding with the help of a Christian friend; the people of the village think she has drowned herself.[9]

Some time later, as Faber is shown developing a more responsible view of the matter, he muses about his own actions:

> He had deposed her idol —the God who she believed could pardon, and the bare belief in whom certainly could comfort her; he had taken the place with her of that imaginary, yet for some, necessary being;

[9]The scene in which Juliet pleads with Paul to whip her for her past indiscretion leads Woolf to conclude MacDonald is exhibiting sadism (GK, pp. 306-14). He is well answered by Reis: "If the fictional representation of cruelty and violence is to be taken as symptomatic of their presence in the psychic makeup of every author in whose works they appear, what artist is immune to the accusation? For that matter, perhaps none of us is immune, in which case the observation is not worth making" (pp. 59, 60).

but when, in the agony of repentant shame, she looked to him for the pardon he alone could give her, he had turned from her with loathing, contempt, and insult! He was the one in the whole earth, who, by saying to her Let it be forgotten, *could have lifted her into life and hope!*

Faber's action of repelling her, therefore, marks him as a man of low moral and spiritual character. The man with a more God-like character would have acted in a manner more worthy of God's child by extending her the forgiveness that she sorely sought, thereby exemplifying God's willingness to forgive her. MacDonald uses the biblical incident of the adulterous woman forgiven by Christ with "Neither do I condemn thee; go, and sin no more" as a frequent reference throughout this section of the novel.[10]

The full hypocrisy of Faber's action, however, is now revealed to the reader: he discovers in town his own illegitimate daughter, the offspring of a previous affair with another woman, of whom he had lost track. Encountering the child is the first incident that brings Faber to a true realization of the duplicity of his position, and from that time on he begins to move toward moral and spiritual enlightenment. In hiding, Juliet bears their own child, and in a scene that is strained by coincidence, Faber is called to minister to her in a room kept dark so that he does not recognize her.

But the discovery is made at the opportune time, and the couple is reconciled. In their child there is further expression of the divine mystery of life that is ready to bring them to a fuller knowledge of their true nature before God: "He and she met in that child's life — her being was the eternal fact of their unity. . . . Both she and he had to learn that there was yet a closer bond between them, necessary indeed to the fact that a child *could* be born of them, namely that they two had issued from the one perfect Heart of love." Their child, the fruit of their love, should become a powerful symbol to them of the

[10]John 8:11.

Love that is at the very core of the universe, and that loves all men into being. Thus, although each previously had failed to guide the other to truth, the experience of having a child offers them another opportunity to discover life's true grace, because the divine love continually flows in all the core experiences of life. All of life is sacramental.

CONCLUSION

Perhaps the single strongest impression one takes away from the novels is that of the depth and scope of MacDonald's sacramentalism. All natural phenomena and all experiences in life are associated with the divine love and have a constant potential to be means of grace. The experiences which befall man because he too is a natural being — birth, procreation, death — are sacred, and should be sources of joy, simply because God is expressing Himself and His nature in them. If man does not respond properly to these experiences, it is because he is not reading God's intentions correctly and is not being obedient to the divine will. At a time when such novelists as Samuel Butler and Thomas Hardy were opposing the idea of revealed religious truth, and were thinking darkly on man's lot in a universe that seemed to them capricious and malignant, MacDonald was depicting man as capable of benefiting greatly from the inherent truth of things if he used the opportunities given him.

But in MacDonald's world man is often guilty of ignoring God's presence and true intentions. Not recognizing God in His works, he exploits life's experiences for the pleasure and profit of the self. But man must be saved from his various "false selves." Either these fill him with a sense of pride and imagined self-sufficiency, or they (e.g., the rational self) contrive false explanations for the phenomena of life based upon mere sensual experience or appearances. The man who awakens to the true nature of things nurtures the growth of his true self, a process invariably accompanied by his coming into harmony with nature.

For stirring examples of man's directly receiving God's grace through communion with nature, one need only turn to the scenes in *The Marquis of Lossie* in which Malcolm walks by the seashore or through the woods in the moonlight, or those in *Robert Falconer* in which Robert travels through the continent, or those in *Wilfrid Cumbermede* in which Wilfrid is lost in awe among the ice caves of the Swiss Alps. The divine essence of man's being is aroused and nourished as quickly by this communion as by any other means. MacDonald is capable of describing nature vividly and exactly, and his spirit exults in depicting the Wordsworthian harmony that exists between a spiritually responsive character and the natural handiwork of his God.[11]

The novels, then, present us with a vision of life and its meaning which, in its basic analysis, is very much like that of the fantasies. Beneath the complexities of experience MacDonald saw the presence of certain basic patterns, patterns which not only lend structure to his writings but also express the nature of God and His divine grace. Having noted all this, the reader is in a better position to read appreciatively what remains today the most popular of MacDonald's writings: his fairy tales.

[11]Referring to depictions of natural disasters, Reis writes: "In these scenes, the habitual diffuseness of MacDonald's style gives way to a precision of description, a vigor of expression, as effective as that of any of the masters of English narrative—among whom MacDonald is not ordinarily to be counted" (p. 60).

CHAPTER SEVEN

Shadows, Shadows,
Shadows All!

*"Everyone, however, who feels the story, will read its
meaning after his own nature and development: one man
will read one meaning in it, another will read another."*
—Preface to the 1893 American edition of *The Light Princess
and Other Fairy Tales*

I n the fairy story "The Golden Key," at the moment when
Tangle comes into the presence of the Old Man of the Fire,
we read:

> But the moment she stood upright she had a marvellous sense that she
> was in the secret of the earth and all its ways. Everything she had
> seen, or learned from books; all that her grandmother had said or sung
> to her; all the talk of the beasts, birds, and fishes; all that had happened
> to her on her journey with Mossy, and since then in the heart of the
> earth with the Old man and the Older man —all was plain: she
> understood it all, and saw that everything meant the same thing,
> though she could not have put it into words again.

Students of mythology tell us that the effects a religious man
feels in the presence of his myths are similar to those described
in this passage. Tangle is on her way to the land "from whence
the shadows fell"—that is, the land of ultimate reality. The

imagined world of myth is a world that transcends profane time and space; it is the real world of being, where ultimate meaning resides and from which it comes. This meaning has an awful unity to it: it shines through the complexities of things, reconciling contradictory elements, and revealing an essential simplicity, a conformity of import and purpose.

In our story, Tangle has arrived at that place and moment in which "all was plain" — all of her past experiences have become meaningful to her. And this meaning which she perceives has a breath taking unity to it: she "saw that everything meant the same thing." To perceive this unity is one thing; to express it in words is quite another. Tangle found she could not have put her perceptions "into words again."

Such is the nature and power of myth. Two types of myth exist: the ancient folk myths, emerging from the dream-time of man's prehistoric consciousness, and modern literary myths, composed in historic time by men who possess mythic vision and command a mythic style. George MacDonald stands prominently among such writers.

This mythic quality strongly shapes the adult and young people's fantasies considered in prior chapters; it also shapes the fairy stories, but less apparently. Perhaps it is because the fairy stories do have the sheer entertainment of children as an important purpose that the mythic element in them is generally more subdued. The former works are more serious, direct, and forceful, whereas the latter are lighter, more playful, with the elements of absurdity nearer the surface, and fresh breakthroughs into the truth more rare. A startling exception occurs in "The Golden Key," which we will consider shortly; but basically the fairy stories have less depth than MacDonald's other works, and can be briefly discussed.

An additional reason for briefly discussing the fairy tales is that their themes have been presented more compellingly to the adult mind in the longer fantasies; the fairy tales dilute and simplify these themes so that children can understand them. This can be illustrated by juxtaposing the fairy story "The Giant's

Heart" and the episode of the wooden men who oppose the little girl trying to grow wings in Chapter Twenty-three of *Phantastes*. We discussed in some detail the incident of wooden men in our chapter on *Phantastes*. The theme in both stories is similar: true children of God can receive serious spiritual harm from "good churchmen" whose humanity has been seriously distorted because of the religious attitudes they have acquired from the institutionalized church. The counterpart of the wooden men in this fairy tale is the giant who has given his heart to an eagle to care for in her far-off nest. " 'It's a fretting care to have a heart of one's own to look after,' " he complains to his wife. " 'The responsibility is too much for me.' " As an evidence of his debased moral and spiritual state, he crassly fattens little children and eats them like radishes.

The little girl and boy featured in the tale, Tricksey-Wee and Buffy-Bob, wander into Giantland and find their own lives threatened by the giant. They try to set things right by learning from the birds of the wood where the giant's heart is being kept. Then they make the perilous journey to the eagle's nest atop Mount Skycrack, helped by a horde of obliging spiders. Having retrieved the heart, they return it to the giant only after he promises to be better. But the giant reneges on his promise, and the tale ends with little Buffy-Bob felling him with his trusty pocketknife.

The moral is clear: one should keep his heart in his own charge, and not trust another with its nurture. To be lazy, as the giant is, and place it in another's care is morally reprehensible, and results in destroying one's own humanity. One notes with interest that Mount Skycrack is described as looming in the distance "like the spire of a church. . . ." The parallel suggested between the mountain, with its imposing eagle as caretaker, and the institutionalized church is strengthened as one recalls MacDonald's general attitude toward the church, and his unhappiness with its shortcomings. To abandon one's heart to its care is a prescription for spiritual retrogression. Thus the tale makes a point very similar to that made by the incident of the wooden men in *Phantastes*, but here it is generally diluted, the focus being more upon the story and its entertainment value. One does not feel the imaginative strength of statement that made the longer adult fantasy so powerful.

The tale of the giant's heart is one of many fairy tales which first appeared in the somewhat curious novel *Adela Cathcart*. In this novel MacDonald offers an interesting theory of the moral nature and purpose of the fairy tale—and of all imaginative literature that springs from a truly Christian imagination. The work contains within a framework of realistic narrative a number of experiments in symbolic tales, from fairy story to various moral anecdotes to parable. The plot cleverly allows their telling. A group of relatives and friends gather in Colonel Cathcart's country home during the Christmas holidays, but their merriment is curtailed by his daughter Adela's strange illness, for which no medical remedy has been found. A new doctor is summoned, a young man of unorthodox medical notions, who feels that her ailment is spiritual rather than physical. He proposes a remedy of storytelling, whereby the group meets on appointed evenings and listens to the contribution of one of its various members.

The cure is wondrously successful. Adela not only is cured, but in the end marries the doctor. MacDonald speculates in the novel that all disease ultimately has a moral source, inasmuch as man belongs to a fallen race; hence, individuals who are ill may often profit more from moral and spiritual ministrations than from physical ones. The imagination is indispensable to this kind of aid, because it can present a vision of truth necessary for spiritual well-being. (MacDonald's view of the nature and function of the imagination will be presented more thoroughly in the closing chapter.)

Two other of MacDonald's stories that are often included in collections of his fairy tales appear in *Adela Cathcart*. Seeing them in the context of that novel proves helpful in understanding them. One is "The Light Princess," which is the first story to be told to the ailing Adela, a model demonstration of MacDonald's theory of the salutary effect of a good tale. But he begins his prescription with a gentle dose. The story is indeed one of the "lightest" MacDonald ever wrote, filled as it is with punning, and characterized by a generally pixyish tone. The theme is similar to that of the story of Cosmo in *Phantastes:* true love is self-giving; one must die to live.

SACRAMENTALISM IN THE FAIRY TALES

The other of the more familiar fairy tales that first appeared in *Adela Cathcart* is "The Shadows." The theme is in harmony with MacDonald's sacramental view of nature and circumstances, considering as it does the good moral effect that shadows have upon people's consciences. The story concerns a sick old man who in delirium has a vision of fairies taking him to the Land of Shadows. There he learns of the many ways in which, in this world, shadows have helped men achieve moral and spiritual growth. They frighten people during moments of wrong doing, thus lessening the amount of evil in the world.

MacDonald's sacramentalism is also a significant element in his fairy story, "Little Daylight," which appears in the middle of *At the Back of the North Wind* (previously discussed). This story develops the theme that evil finally results in good: the heroine finally breaks free of an evil fairy's curse, finding herself a stronger and better person because of it.

One of the poorer of the fairy tales is "The Day Boy and the Night Girl." Its theme, the sacramental effects of nature, is developed by its focus on man's relationship to nature, at night under the aegis of the moon, and during the day under the aegis of the sun. A large part of the difficulty with one story is the uncertainty that the reader feels about whether he is in Fairyland or the real world. MacDonald seems to want to talk directly about the real world, but he strives to create a setting in which anything can happen, and uses the same license that he does in the pure fairy tales. The result is a disturbing offense to the reader's sense of reality.

The plot concerns a witch, Watho, who raises two children

in two different ways: a boy, Photogen, so that he is aware only of day, thinking it the only reality; and a girl, Nycteris, so that she is aware only of the night, in turn thinking it the only reality. How Photogen discovers the night and Nycteris the day, and their correspondingly fresh and wonderful new ways of seeing the world, occupies most of the story. When Nycteris escapes into the night, leaving the perpetual darkness of the cave in Watho's castle where she was raised, she is rapturously delighted with the wonders of nature under the moon. On the other hand, Photogen, familiar only with daylight, is very frightened when he first discovers darkness. But the two meet one night, and Nycteris helps Photogen to orient himself to the night as he helps her to know the delights of the day. Together they also kill the witch Watho and inherit her castle. The story ends with their anticipating a still greater day to come, thus emphasizing — as so many of the fairy stories do — that sense of progress toward a higher experience of life.

TRIUMPH OVER EVIL

Indeed, MacDonald's fairies seem to be more often evil than good, with their machinations being foiled in an entertaining manner. He is generally careful to integrate whatever moral intentions he has in a particular story with its aesthetic structure, so that the effect is seldom preachy. A good example is the tale "The Carasoyn," which works obliquely with the theme of becoming.

The rather complex plot concerns a shepherd boy, Colin, and the difficulties he encounters because of a horde of fairies. Twice he falls prey to their chicaneries, once as a boy and later as a grown man. In order to extricate himself from each predicament, he must perform a task outlined for him by an old woman, a figure not unlike the great-grandmother of the Curdie stories. She can only be found when the seeker loses himself — a variation of the dying-to-live theme.

Colin undertakes the first task the old woman assigns him in order to free a little girl the fairies are holding prisoner. He must obtain a bottle of a rare Carasoyn wine for the Queen of the Fairies. When he delivers it to the eager queen and she drinks of it, she and her company suddenly become aged and wrinkled. (Carasoyn wine is only for really good people, we are told; hence, it ages the evil fairies.) Here is an interesting recurrence of another theme from the Curdie stories. One recalls how the old queen Irene, so glorious in her appearance to Curdie and his father, was Old Mother Wotherwop to the coarse-minded miners. Only people who have grown to be good themselves can recognize and appreciate what is truly good; to the wicked, too large a good may have bad effects, because it is too far beyond the grasp of their current moral state. As depicted in Curdie's experience with the fire of roses, good may be immediately terrible.

Colin's second adventure with the fairies occurs when he is a man. Having married the girl whom he previously rescued from the fairies, he loses his child to them in a kidnapping. He performs a similar task at the instruction of the same old woman, finds the fairies, and rescues his son — but this time Colin extracts a sworn promise from them not to annoy his family again. And thus the story closes: the evil fairies have been foiled, their activities having accomplished no permanent harm to man, and those characters who have been extricated from their power are better beings, it is implied, because of their encounters.

Colin triumphs because of his courage and his determination to help those in distress. Another story that gives an intriguing presentation of this theme is "Cross Purposes," a story that is more symmetrical than most of MacDonald's tales. The narrative opens with the Queen of Fairyland commissioning a fairy and a goblin, Peasebottom and Toadstool, to bring two mortals to her domain for her entertainment. Peasebottom entices a girl named Alice to make the trip; she is a spoiled little girl who is bored with her life and desires to leave home to follow the sunset. Toadstool brings Richard, a Curdie-like little boy whose poverty, it is implied, has molded him into a boy of solid and

promising character. Alice and Richard meet enroute to Fairyland, and both have second thoughts about their journey. Since
fairies are rendered powerless against mortals as soon as the
mortals exercise their wills against the fairies' schemes, Peasebottom and Toadstool disappear, and Alice and Richard are left
to find their way back home on their own.

They are, of course, lost. As Richard heroically tries to befriend Alice, she rebuffs him, sullen and snobbish. In their ensuing
adventures, however, she finds that to withdraw from Richard
envelops her in a frightening loneliness, so that she comes to feel
that "there was no one in the universe but herself." Coming to
her wits' end, she runs to Richard for help. This little incident,
swiftly drawn, depicts that turning point in the moral experience
of people that MacDonald speaks of on numerous occasions,
both in his sermons and in his novels. It is the experience that,
he deeply hopes, all men who are growing morally worse, retrogressing on the scale of becoming, will have sooner or later,
in this world or another. The definitive depiction of this idea
occurs in *Lilith*, in the scene in which Vane meets the skeletons
in the nether world: the loneliness and silence of darkness, in
which the hellish fantasies of the depraved individuals' tormented
souls have free reign, are the ultimate goad to his turning. In
the fairy tale Alice has but the slightest taste of all this.

Richard, who has fallen in love with Alice, gladly befriends
her. In the darkness he is excited when he thinks that her face
gives off light by which he can see the path. But MacDonald
explains what is actually happening: "The fact was, that the
moment he began to love Alice, his eyes began to send forth
light. What he thought came from Alice's face, really came from
his eyes. All about her and her path he could see, and every
minute saw better; but to his own path he was blind." This little
occurrence intriguingly suggests the nature and power of love:
love enables a person to see another sympathetically, and to help
him. The result is that Alice begins to have a similar experience,
thinking that Richard's face lights the path, and because each

sees the other's path clearly, they get on well. Love exercised kindles a responsive love, and a way opens in the darkness.

Finding home, however, is not easy. In a passage in which MacDonald uses the "anything-can-happen" quality of dreams to give us a convincing experience of the unexpected that may continually occur in Fairyland, Richard and Alice face several baffling difficulties. The two overcome each one by an act of defiant courage. They finally see each other as far apart — on opposite sides of a great chasm, many feet across, with the gap between them many feet deep. In their distress Richard decides this too is a trick, and when both jump courageously toward the other, they discover what appeared to be a great expanse is only a gap a foot or two wide and deep. As a reward for their courage the Queen of Fairyland grants them free and unmolested passage to her realm whenever they please.

The process of spiritual becoming, which is depicted in Alice's experience, has a more thorough presentation in the longer fairy story "The Wise Woman." The plot focuses upon two girls: Rosamond, a princess, and Agnes, a shepherd's daughter. Both are seriously spoiled by their parents, so that each becomes very conceited. This moral ugliness brings each in turn to encounters with the Wise Woman who lives in the wood, a figure not unlike Queen Irene in the Curdie stories. Through various experiences with her, both girls learn self-discipline and humility. Much of the charm of the story lies in its consistent blend of playfulness and seriousness, together with its strongly realistic depiction of the slow, agonizing process whereby moral lessons are learned and virtue is acquired. The transformations are not facile: they are as preciously achieved as those of real life. Though Mac-Donald's narrator in "The Wise Woman" playfully insists that the fairyland of the story is a very different type of world from our own, the reader concludes that the import of experiences in both worlds is very much the same.

LONGING FOR FAIRYLAND

Consistently in MacDonald's fantasies, to achieve admittance to Fairyland is a prize that answers a deep longing in men's hearts.

Shadows, Shadows, Shadows All!

Fairyland, a realm in the imagination, is a type of intermediate world between the world we know and the world of man's ultimate destination. It is a higher world, a world of glory and wonder. People of different spiritual sensitivities and needs arrive by different routes, and often became fit for the atmosphere by receiving there a fuller portion of life than they have in this world. These ideas are presented with great appeal in "The Golden Key," the finest of the fairy tales.

The boy and girl in this story are named Mossy and Tangle. Mossy finds a fascinating golden key at the foot of a glorious rainbow, and sets out in quest of the lock which it will open. He is joined in his quest by Tangle, a little girl from the same village. They meet in the cottage of a wise old woman (another of a considerable company of such figures in the fantasies and fairy tales), who cleanses and refreshes them and directs them on their way.

MacDonald's belief in the upward mobility of all life, with all living things becoming freer and more beautiful as they grow in spiritual wisdom, is charmingly set forth in the incident of the fish-like creatures of the lady's cottage. They act as messengers, bringing the children to her cottage and generally doing her bidding, while waiting expectantly for the day when they will be eaten by the people of Fairyland. That is their ambition, for it is "their highest end in that condition." But this consummation is not their final end: they arise phoenix-like from the fire upon which they have been prepared — creatures with a more glorious incarnation — and are released to a larger freedom.

Leaving the old lady's cottage, Mossy and Tangle travel through a strange valley filled only with intriguing shadows, and they long to find "the country whence the shadows fell." The valley vaguely suggests this present world seen from a Platonic point of view: its substances are only shadows. The children's journey through it makes them age, Mossy's hair becoming streaked with grey, and Tangle developing wrinkles in her forehead. As they reach the borders of the valley, Tangle loses Mossy in a poignant little scene that suggests all the pathos of that moment when an aged person loses his life's mate. Each then goes on his way alone, separately meeting, after various difficulties, the Old Man of the Sea. Tangle meets him first, and then goes on to meet two other figures, the Old Man of the Earth and the still older Old Man of the Fire. The latter is able to direct her to "the country whence the shadows fell," where all the characters of the story long to go.

Tangle's meeting with the Old Man of the Fire is one of the most fascinating passages in the entirety of MacDonald's writings. To Tangle's wonder, she finds him to be like "a marvellous Child" engaged in a mysterious game "of infinite meaning," and we recognize him as a surrogate for God himself. MacDonald is at his suggestive best in a descriptive passage that must speak for itself:

> There was such an awfulness of absolute repose on the face of the child that Tangle stood dumb before him. He had no smile, but the love in his large grey eyes was deep as the centre. And with the repose there lay on his face a shimmer as of moonlight, which seemed as if any moment it might break into such a ravishing smile as would cause the beholder to weep himself to death. But the smile never came, and the moonlight lay there unbroken. For the heart of the child was too deep for any smile to reach from it to his face.

A reader who knows MacDonald's sermons is reminded of the one entitled "A Child in the Midst," in which MacDonald argues that of all the comparisons one can make between God and man, God is most like the essence of ideal childhood. God is no "great King on a grand throne, thinking how grand he is, and making it the business of his being and the end of his universe to keep up his glory." Rather, ". . . he alone can be perfectly, abandonedly simple and devoted. . . . It is his childlikeness that makes him our God and Father." The sermon gives the concept compelling exposition; the powerful myth of the fairy tale presents to our imaginations the beauty of the truth itself.[1]

Tangle's route differs from the one Mossy takes. His golden

[1] *US* I.

key in hand, he proceeds by a different way to meet the Old Man of the Sea. Because Mossy's feet are very weary, he receives a bath in the Old Man's inner cave, and is wondrously refreshed. The Old Man explains:

> "You have tasted of death now. . . . Is it good?"
> "It is good," said Mossy. "It is better than life."
> "No," said the Old Man: "it is only more life. Your feet will make no holes in the water now."

Thus enabled to continue his journey atop the waves of the sea, he comes to a great precipice of rock, and climbing halfway up, he is momentarily stopped by an impassable cliff, until he sees in the face of the rock a small keyhole surrounded with sapphires. The key fits, the rock barrier falls away, and Mossy climbs a rainbow stair into Tangle's presence. They happily discover that they both are now beings of great beauty and nobility, "younger and better, stronger and wiser, than they had ever been before." Together they joyously climb the rainbow with its riotous splendor of color, moving toward the "country whence the shadows fall."

The careful reader is always wary of taking a symbolic tale too far in the direction of allegory, hunting for precise meanings when meaning is suggested only in the general pattern and occasional elements of the story. One cannot help but be intrigued, however, by the different routes Mossy and Tangle must take between their parting and their reunion at the foot of the rainbow. It is Mossy who has the golden key, which seems to be a symbol of the imagination in its capacity to envision and desire eternity. Mossy's imagination was nurtured and exercised in his youth in a manner MacDonald advocates in his novels and essays when he theorizes about how children are to be educated imaginatively. As a child, Mossy learned of the existence of the golden key from his great-aunt while listening to her stories. He earned his name by his habit of sitting all day long upon a moss-covered stone, reading stories. In the process, his innate desire for a higher and better world grew strong.

The Harmony Within • George MacDonald

It may be helpful to recall Wordsworth's famous lines from *The Prelude* in a passage from Book VI, in which he describes the function of the imagination as establishing within man the certainty of his immortality:

> Our destiny, our being's heart and home,
> Is with infinitude, and only there;
> With hope it is, hope that can never die,
> Effort, and· expectation, and desire,
> And something evermore about to be.

It is the imagination that enables man to see beyond the immediate to the eternal, establishing the conviction that his destiny is "only there." To cultivate this aspect of his being is to further the realization of his desire. Mossy's key, respected by all the characters he meets, shortens his journey through the nether world and gains him easy access to his destination.

Tangle, on the other hand, who has no key, must travel a longer, more tedious route to the same destination. As a child she was less fortunate than Mossy: she was "neglected and left untidy." Frightened into Fairyland by mischievous fairies (who thereby inadvertently do her great good), she has a longer interview in the Wise Woman's cottage than does Mossy, and her general progress through the nether world is slower. After meeting the Old Man of the Sea she must visit the Old Man of the Earth, and then the Old Man of the Fire. On her way to the latter she passes through a scorching fire that seems more than she can bear; after her meeting with the Old Man of the Fire (described above), a serpent leads her to her destination. One is inclined to see in these events indications that Tangle's route — that of the more unimaginative and less fortunate individual — is one by which wisdom is gained from more direct experiences with evil, and holiness is acquired from a more direct purging.

Interesting and profitable comparisons may be drawn between this story and the closing chapters of *Lilith,* in which the party of characters there make "the journey home" to the Father of the Universe. MacDonald's achievement in creating an aura that

Shadows, Shadows, Shadows All!

answers longings deep within the heart of good men, an aura that suggests abounding joy and an ever-increasing good upon the upward journey of life, scarcely has its peer in this type of literature. "The Golden Key" is a masterpiece in literary myth.

CHAPTER EIGHT

Showing the Unshowable

"Law is the soil in which alone beauty will grow; beauty is the only stuff in which Truth can be clothed; and you may, if you will, call Imagination the tailor that cuts her garments to fit her. . . ."
— Preface to the 1893 American edition of *The Light Princess and Other Fairy Tales*

Today, many who think about the relation of Christianity to art discern an incompatibility between them. They see art, by its very nature, as having to be free and unconstrained by dogma, and Christianity as arbitrary and confining. Such people would be quick to see MacDonald as a man torn between two worlds. Having failed as a minister in the established church, he turned to his second love, imaginative writing, and attempted to reconcile it to his purpose, using it as a substitute for the pulpit. His true artistic talent, struggling for breath under a great blanket of dogma, is all but stifled.

But it must be observed that any man's art bears deepest relation to his view of the meaning of life, whether he intends it that way or not. No artist's work can exist apart from his faith, whether his belief be Christian or otherwise. In MacDonald's system of belief, nothing is more compatible, nothing is more unified in nature, intent, and purpose, than art and faith.

Showing the Unshowable

As he states in the above epigraph, "Beauty is the only stuff in which Truth can be clothed," and the imagination cuts the clothes. Any deficiencies in his art may point to deficiencies in the quality of his imaginative talent, but do not indicate that his faith has diminished that talent.

CHIEF INFLUENCES

The chief influences shaping MacDonald's view of the nature and function of the imagination appear to be three: German Romanticism, Coleridge, and certain Christian mystics such as Swedenborg. Evidently MacDonald discovered the German Romantics during his college days. He was already at that time skeptical of the capacity of Calvinism — or of any strict, logical system of abstractions — to contain truth. The Germans — E. T. W. Hoffmann and Friedrich von Hardenberg (Novalis) were his favorites — taught that truth was first received by the imagination and the intuition, and then rationally apprehended. This apparently confirmed what he already felt to be true. After all, did not the ancient Hebrew prophets, such as Ezekiel, for instance, present the reader with visions to be interpreted rather than with systems of thought to be learned by rote? Did not biblical writers in general present depictions of human experience in narrative form rather than arguments derived from abstract systems of thought?

Coleridge was another strong influence on MacDonald. Stephen Prickett points out how closely MacDonald's theory and practice derive from that of Coleridge, and what type of additions MacDonald makes. The central framework for Coleridge's thought is that of the existence of two worlds: the "I am" and the "It is," the subjective and the objective. Symbols bring these two worlds together in reciprocal relationship, and the poet's imagination is a symbolizing faculty. Coleridge celebrated the character of Scripture because of the manner in which these two realms of meaning seemed to him to coincide in its narratives: "In the Scriptures therefore both facts and persons must of necessity have a two-fold significance, a past and a future, a temporary and a perpetual, a particular and a universal application. They must be at once Portraits and Ideals."[1] In much of his poetry, such as *The Ancient Mariner,* he sought to incorporate these two realms.

Similarly, MacDonald's fantasies present us with two worlds, interrelated and intermingling — our immediate physical world and the imagined realm of Faerie. Faerie overlays the "real" world of our own experience, and, through a system of symbolic correspondences, achieves a clarifying reciprocity with it. As we have noted elsewhere, the mysticism in MacDonald's theory of correspondences comes most probably from Swedenborg, with additions from Boehme, Blake, and Law. This union of mysticism and Coleridge's thought, combined with the strong influence of German Romanticism, enabled MacDonald to bring a fresh approach to his Evangelical-pietistic concerns.

VIEW OF THE IMAGINATION

These influences not only firmly convinced MacDonald that the imagination is essential to the apprehension of spiritual truth, but also led him to develop a theory for this belief. In his essay "The Imagination: Its Functions and Its Culture," printed in *Orts,* MacDonald writes: ". . . we dare to claim for the true, childlike humble imagination, such an inward oneness with the laws of the universe that it possesses itself an insight into the very nature of things." He continues to argue that man's imagination must be co-laborer with his intellect; otherwise his thinking is merely analytic and sterile.

In this co-laboring, MacDonald concludes, the primary function of the imagination is to give forms to thought. These forms are not original with man, however; they come from nature, which God has made. In fact, God is constantly in the process of creating both nature and man himself: all things, man included,

[1]*The Statesman's Manual,* as quoted in Prickett, p. 18.

are presently being thought by God. Hence, when man thinks imaginatively, he is thinking God's thoughts after Him.

Further, since God continues to think the forms of nature, He is constantly investing them with meaning. All of them mean man well — they are sacramental. Man, thinking imaginatively, will come to know some of these meanings when he is morally and spiritually in harmony with God. The quotation above stipulates that the imagination must be "true, childlike," and "humble." What MacDonald means by these qualities, and how essential he feels them to be, we have discussed throughout this book. It should be unnecessary to point out that he is not talking about any undisciplined imagination, let alone a deliberately evil one.

MacDonald's view of the extent to which insightful thinking depends upon God is perhaps made more clear by a poem he wrote, entitled "A Cry":

> Lord, hear my discontent: all blank I stand,
> A mirror polished by thy hand;
> Thy sun's beams flash and flame from me —
> I cannot help it: here I stand, there he!
> To one of them I cannot say,
> Go, and on yonder water play;
> Nor one poor ragged daisy can I fashion —
> I do not make the words of this my limping passion!
> If I should say, Now I will think a thought,
> Lo, I must wait, unknowing
> What thought in me is growing,
> Until the thing to birth be brought!
> Nor know I then what next will come
> From out the gulf of silence dumb:
> I am the door the thing will find
> To pass into the general mind!
> I cannot say I think —
> I only stand upon the thought-well's brink:
> From darkness to the sun the water bubbles up —
> I lift it in my cup.

The Harmony Within • George MacDonald

Thou only thinkest —I am thought;
Me and my thought thou thinkest. Naught
Am I but as a fountain spout
From which thy water welleth out.
Thou art the only one, the all in all. —
Yet when my soul on thee doth call
And thou dost answer out of everywhere,
I in thy allness have my perfect share. [2]

God is all in all. The true man delights in this truth; the false man cringes in its presence, striving to maintain his sense of autonomy, as Lilith does when she encounters Mara. In the above poem, MacDonald waits with childlike expectancy before God, convinced that the very formulation of his thoughts is from God. The precise thoughts God can give any man are those appropriate to his spiritual state at the time. MacDonald's views may seem to some to be completely fatalistic, but what keeps them from being so in his mind is the freedom of man's will to obey God's precepts and thus grow into a higher state of being, or conversely, to revel in supposed autonomy, thus sinking still further in the scale of being toward "the animals' country," as we noted previously. Because man is free in his willed responses to God's precepts, he may be said to will his own thoughts, indirectly.

God is, of course, entirely benevolent and trustworthy, ever working for man's spirtual growth. But He honors man's free decisions, and a man's will does control the *quality* of thoughts he receives. If a man wills to keep his mind and imagination clean, God may be trusted to give him an appreciable amount of truth. MacDonald's insistence upon the freedom of the will, with the blend he achieves between the two imponderables of

[2]Manlove quotes selected lines from "A Cry" and, after considering certain aspects of MacDonald's theory, complains of his trying to "have it both ways," of being "simultaneously 'chaotic' and responsible" (p. 66). He then proceeds to find fault with both levels of MacDonald's art. He appears unwilling to allow MacDonald his view concerning the role that God plays in man's being and in his world. MacDonald assumes the complete trustworthiness of God.

divine sovereignty and human responsibility, is not unlike Augustine's.

MacDonald also believed that the thoughts God gives the artist, expressed in their appropriate beauty in art, have an especial power to arouse virtuous feelings in his readers. This, too, is an idea derived from Novalis, who in his tale *Heinrich von Ofterdingen* teaches that the true spirit of fable and the spirit of virtue are the same, and the former ministers to the latter. A good illustration of this principle can be found in *Phantastes.* When Anodos, in obedience to the woman of the cottage with the four doors, leaves to perform a noble deed, he is commissioned to help the two brothers to rid their father's land of the three giants who are despoiling it. Anodos's mandate is to sing his songs to them, which arouse the brothers to virtuous and valorous actions. Clearly, the songs, or the art they represent, have the power to inspire good deeds. One recalls as well the power of song in the Curdie stories. MacDonald's belief in this power must have been a strong factor in enabling him to leave the pastorate and devote his life to literary creation.

INCOHERENCE AND UNDERLYING MEANING

In both worlds of man's experience — the "I am" and the "It is" — MacDonald perceived both a surface incoherence and an underlying meaning. In his imaginative prose writings he undertook to incorporate each of these, and to penetrate the incoherence with the meanings he saw, an undertaking that he felt required a certain spiritual maturity. Again, he found his authority in Novalis.

Phantastes is prefaced with a three-paragraph epigraph taken from Novalis's theories on the nature of the fairy tale, or *Marchen* (translated from the German), which presents the following principles. A fairy tale is like a dream-picture without coherence, a story controlled by association that has only a general allegorical meaning. But in the tale all of nature must express the entire world of the spirit. The world of the fairy-tale must be entirely different from, and yet at the same time bear a similarity to, the true world, as chaos is similar to creation. It must also have a musical harmony. This, in summary, appears to be the basic literary theory that shaped *Phantastes* and all of MacDonald's succeeding fantasies, and what accounts for their primary characteristics: the surface incoherence, the dream-like quality, the generalized symbolical intention, the relationships between the world of nature and the world of spirit and the musical orchestration of themes.[3]

This combination of a surface incoherence with an underlying harmony characterizes both the outer world and the world of the mind, and is properly to be mirrored in the worlds of the imagination created by art. The "harmony within," the hidden unity and coherence of all things is with God, whose meanings and purposes infuse the entirety of this apparent chaos with a higher order. The spiritually mature artist is able to catch glimpses of the true import of things. The glory of God's purposes is such that, when at last they are more fully revealed to those capable of receiving the revelation, the recipients will be satisfied in awe.

It bears repeating at this point that MacDonald never claims for himself the spiritual maturity that is, in his system of thought, the *sine qua non* for complete understanding; he is singularly free from the cultic mentality. To him, pontificating would be certain evidence that the inferior self — the death of which is the prime essential to spiritual health — is very much alive and well; hence, anyone with such an attitude would be patently deluding himself.

CONCLUSION

Such, then, is the general blend of literary and theological convictions that shaped George MacDonald's fictional worlds. MacDonald wants the incidents to both baffle his readers and

[3]See Woolf, *GK*, pp. 42ff, for an account of a misprint in this epigraph — the word for *inconsistency* was given as *consistency* — due to a mistake in MacDonald's source. But, as Woolf observes, MacDonald must have read Novalis correctly, although his proofreading apparently was faulty.

make a certain sense to them, as events in the actual world of human experience did to him. One would expect that any author undertaking this sort of task would at times produce material that is unduly private in character and import — and Mac-Donald's work is sometimes just that. In addition, a disturbing amount of his work, though it has virtue in abundance, lacks an aesthetically pleasing art form; MacDonald wrote too quickly and too prolifically to be as careful a stylist as he should have been. Nevertheless, MacDonald's best attempts in literary myth, of which "The Golden Key" is an example, have genuine power. This power comes partly from the conviction he succeeds in arousing within his readers that he is exploring spiritual experience in an imaginatively significant manner.

Successful myths rise to probe the ultimate mysteries of existence, simultaneously arousing the reader's wonder and awakening in him a desire that these insights be true. The reader becomes convinced that they bring him into closer proximity to the Ultimate Mystery, which stands considerably beyond the reach of any system of abstract principles discursively offered, and that he is receiving foreknowledge of a world the likes of which he will one day enter himself. In his better fantasies MacDonald's writing has this effect. He felt that creating literary myths was the happiest method of imaginatively exploring and communicating his deeply held religious convictions. In so doing, he projected imagined worlds that have a "harmony within," that answer some of man's deepest curiosities and desires, and, through the power of myth, show the unshowable. It is in this mythopoeic art that he excels, an achievement that makes him deserving of a prominent place in any listing of literary mythmakers.

SELECTED BIBLIOGRAPHY

Two helpful bibliographies are, first, the one contained in Greville MacDonald's biography *George MacDonald and His Wife* (London: George Allen & Unwin, 1924); and, second, John Malcolm Bulloch's "Bibliography of George MacDonald," *Aberdeen University Library Bulletin,* 5, No. 30 (February 1925), 679-747. Bulloch undertakes to trace the several editions of MacDonald's works up to the centenary celebration, a forbidding task because of MacDonald's inclination to revise and regroup his stories in various editions, and because of the wide pirating of his works in America. Muriel Hutton has offered minor corrections of Bulloch's work in "Sour Grapeshot: Fault-finding in *A Centennial Bibliography of George MacDonald,*" *Aberdeen University Review,* 41, No. 134 (Autumn 1965), 85-88. Following is a list of his chief titles.

PRIMARY SOURCES

Adela Cathcart. London: Hurst & Blackett, 1864.
Alec Forbes of Howglen. London: Hurst & Blackett, 1865.
Annals of a Quiet Neighbourhood. London: Hurst & Blackett, 1867.
At the Back of the North Wind. London: Strahan, 1871.
A Book of Strife in the Form of a Diary of an Old Soul. London: Unwin Brothers, 1880.
Castle Warlock. London: Sampson Low, 1882.
David Elginbrod. London: Hurst & Blackett, 1863.
Dealings with Fairies. London: Strahan, 1867.
Donal Grant. London: Kegan Paul, 1883.
A Dish of Orts: Chiefly Papers on the Imagination, and on Shakespeare. Enl. ed. London, 1893.
The Elect Lady. London: Kegan Paul, 1888.
England's Antiphon. London: Macmillan & Co., 1868.
Exotics: A Translation of the Spiritual Songs of Novalis. London: Strahan, 1876.
The Flight of the Shadow. London: Kegan Paul, 1891.
The Gifts of the Child Christ. London: Sampson Low, 1882.
Guild Court. London: Hurst & Blackett, 1868.
Gutta Percha Willie: The Working Genius. London: King, 1873.
Heather and Snow. London: Chatto & Windus, 1893.
Home Again. London: Kegan Paul, 1887.
The Hope of the Gospel. London: Ward, Lock, Bowden, 1892.
Lilith. London: Chatto & Windus, 1895.
Malcolm. London: King, 1875.

Selected Bibliography

The Marquis of Lossie. London: Hurst & Blackett, 1877.

Mary Marston. London: Sampson Low, 1881.

The Miracles of Our Lord. London: Strahan, 1870.

Paul Faber, Surgeon. London: Hurst & Blackett, 1879.

Phantastes: A Faerie Romance for Men and Women. London: Smith, Elder, 1858.

The Poetical works of George MacDonald. 2 vols. London: Chatto & Windus, 1893.

The Portent. London: Smith, Elder 1864.

The Princess and Curdie. London: Chatto & Windus, 1883.

The Princess and the Goblin. London: Strahan, 1872.

Rampolli. London: Longmans, 1897.

Ranald Bannerman's Boyhood. London: Strahan, 1871.

Robert Falconer. London: Hurst & Blackett, 1868.

A Rough Shaking. London: Blackie, 1891.

St. George and St. Michael. London: King, 1876.

Salted with Fire. London: Hurst & Blackett, 1897.

The Seaboard Parish. London: Tinsley, 1868.

Sir Gibbie. London: Hurst & Blackett, 1879.

There and Back. London: Kegan Paul, 1891.

Thomas Wingfold, Curate. London: Hurst & Blackett, 1876.

The Tragedie of Hamlet. London: Longmans, 1885.

Unspoken Sermons. London: Strahan, 1867.

Unspoken Sermons: Second Series. London: Longmans, 1886.

Unspoken Sermons: Third Series. London: Longmans, 1889.

The Vicar's Daughter. London: Tinsley Brothers, 1872.

Weighed and Wanting. London: Sampson Low, 1882.

What's Mine's Mine. London: Kegan Paul, 1886.

Wilfrid Cumbermede. London: Hurst & Blackett, 1872.

The Wise Woman. London: Strahan, 1875.

SOME RECENT REPRINTS

Alec Forbes of Howglen. Ed. Robert Wolff. New York: Garland, 1975.

At the Back of the North Wind. New York: Garland, 1976.

The Complete Fairy Tales. New York: Schocken, 1977.

Creation in Christ: The Unspoken Sermons. Ed. Rolland Hein. Wheaton, Ill.: Harold Shaw, 1976.

David Elginbrod. Ed. Robert Wolff. New York: Garland, 1975.

The Diary of an Old Soul. Minneapolis: Augsburg, 1975.

A Dish of Orts. Folcroft, Pa.: Folcroft, 1976.

England's Antiphon. Philadelphia: R. West, 1973.

Gifts of the Child Christ. Ed. Glenn Sadler. 2 vols. Grand Rapids, Mich.: Wm. B. Eerdmans, 1973.

The Golden Key. New York: Dell, 1977.

Life Essential: The Hope of the Gospel. Ed. Rolland Hein. Wheaton, Ill.: Harold Shaw, 1976.

The Light Princess. New York: Farrar, Straus and Giroux, 1977.
The Miracles of Our Lord. Ed. Rolland Hein. Wheaton, Ill.: Harold Shaw, 1980.
Paul Faber, Surgeon. Ed. Robert Wolff. New York: Garland, 1975.
Phantastes and Lilith. Grand Rapids, Mich.: Wm. B. Eerdmans, 1964.
The Princess and Curdie. Baltimore: Penguin, 1966.
The Princess and the Goblin. New York: Airmont, 1967.
Robert Falconer. Ed. Robert Wolff. New York: Garland, 1975.
The Wise Woman. New York: Garland, 1976.
The World of George MacDonald: An Anthology of Selections from the Novels. Ed. Rolland Hein. Wheaton, Ill.: Harold Shaw, 1978.

SECONDARY SOURCES

Baker, Joseph Ellis. *The Novel and the Oxford Movement.* Princeton: Princeton University Press, 1932.
Barclay, William. *A Spiritual Autobiography.* Grand Rapids, Mich.: Wm. B. Eerdmans, 1975.
Buckley, Jerome Hamilton. *The Victorian Temper: A Study in Literary Culture.* Cambridge: Harvard University Press, 1951.
Bulloch, John Malcolm. "A Bibliography of George MacDonald." *Aberdeen University Library Bulletin*, 5, No. 30 (February 1925), 679-747.
Fremantle, Anne, ed. *The Visionary Novels of George MacDonald.* New York: Noonday, 1954.
Hetzler, Leo A. "George MacDonald and G.K. Chesterton." *Durham University Journal*, 37 (1976), 176-182.
Hutton, Muriel. "The George MacDonald Collection." *Yale University Library Gazette*, 51 (1976), 74-85.
_____. "Sour Grapeshot: Fault-finding in *A Centennial Bibliography of George MacDonald.*" *Aberdeen University Review*, 41, No. 134 (Autumn 1965), 85-88.
Lewis, C.S. *George MacDonald: An Anthology.* New York: Macmillan, 1948.
_____. *The Great Divorce.* New York: Macmillan, 1952.
_____. *Surprised by Joy: The Shape of My Early LIfe.* London: Geoffrey Bles, 1955.
Liddell, Henry George, and Robert Scott. *A Greek-English Lexicon.* Rev. ed. Oxford: Oxford University Press, 1940.
McGillis, Roderick F. "George MacDonald and the Lilith Legend in the XIX Century." *Mythlore*, 6 (Winter 1979), 3-11.
MacDonald, Greville. *George MacDonald and His Wife.* London: George Allen & Unwin, 1924.
_____. *Reminiscences of a Specialist.* London: George Allen & Unwin, 1932.
MacDonald, Ronald. "George MacDonald," *From a Northern Window.* London: James Nisbet, 1911, pp. 55-113.

Selected Bibliography

Manlove, Colin Nicholas. "George MacDonald's Fairy Tales: Their Roots in MacDonald's Thought." *Studies in Scottish Literature*, 8 (1970), 97-108.

_____. *Modern Fantasy: Five Studies*. Cambridge: Cambridge University Press, 1975.

Morley, Edith J., ed. *Henry Crabb Robinson on Books and Their Writers*. 2 vols. London: Dent, 1938.

Prickett, Stephen. *Romanticism and Religion*. Cambridge: Cambridge University Press, 1976.

_____. *Victorian Fantasy*. Bloomington: Indiana University Press, 1979.

Reis, Richard Herbert. *George MacDonald*. New York: Twayne Publishers, 1972.

Sadler, Glenn. "Cosmic Vision: A Study of the Poetry of George Mac-Donald." Diss. Aberdeen University 1966.

_____, ed. *Gifts of the Child Christ: Fairy Tales and Stories for the Childlike*. Grand Rapids, Mich: Wm. B. Eerdmans, 1973.

Sigman, Joseph. "Death's Ecstasies: Transformation and Rebirth in George MacDonald's *Phantastes*." *English Studies in Canada*, 2, No. 2 (Summer 1976), 203-226.

Walzel, Oskar. *German Romanticism*. New York: Putnam, 1932.

Wolff, Robert Lee. *Gains and Losses: Novels of Faith and Doubt in Victorian England*. New York: Garland, 1977.

_____. *The Golden Key*. New Haven: Yale University Press, 1961.

INDEX

Index

Index

Index